I'm Dysfunctional, You're Dysfunctional

Other books by Wendy Kaminer

A Fearful Freedom
Women Volunteering

I'm Dysfunctional, You're Dysfunctional

The Recovery Movement and Other Self-Help Fashions

WENDY KAMINER

▲▼

Addison-Wesley Publishing Company, Inc.

Reading, Massachusetts ▪ Menlo Park, California ▪ New York
Don Mills, Ontario ▪ Wokingham, England ▪ Amsterdam ▪ Bonn
Sydney ▪ Singapore ▪ Tokyo ▪ Madrid ▪ San Juan
Paris ▪ Seoul ▪ Milan ▪ Mexico City ▪ Taipei

1895

Portions of chapter 1, "Chances Are, You're Codependent Too," and chapter 8, "Conclusion," appeared in *The New York Times Book Review*, February 11, 1990. Reprinted by permission.

Chapter 7, "God Is a Good Parent Too," appeared in *Theology Today*, Fall 1991.

Library of Congress Cataloging-in-Publication Data

Kaminer, Wendy.
    I'm dysfunctional, you're dysfunctional : the recovery movement and other self-help fashions / Wendy Kaminer.
      p. cm.
    Includes bibliographical references and index.
    ISBN 0-201-57062-9
    1. Self-help techniques — United States.
    2. Psychological literature — United States.
    3. Psychology — United States.
    I. Title.
    BF632.K36 1992   91
    158—dc20   CIP

5

Jacket design by Julie Metz
Text design by Diane Levy
Set in 11.5-point Goudy Oldstyle by CopyRight Inc.

3 4 5 6 7 8 9-MW-95949392
Third Printing, June 1992

To my brother Billy

Contents

Acknowledgments

Once again, I have Radcliffe College to thank for providing me with an office and a Harvard ID. Thanks to Pat King and all the staff people at the Schlesinger Library for their friendship and hospitality. Thanks to Barbara Haber for her good humor, conversation, and helpful review of my manuscript. Thanks to William McFeely, as well, for his thoughtful critique.

To my editor, Amy Gash, my agent, Edite Kroll, and to Jane Isay: thanks, of course, for everything.

Introduction

This is not a book about my life or yours. It does not hold the secret to success or salvation. It won't strengthen your self-esteem. I don't think it will get me on "Oprah."

My critique of the recovery movement and other self-help fashions does not reflect my personal experiences (although it surely reflects my temperament). I am not and never have been a convert to recovery or even an occasional consumer of popular psychology, religion, or wellness books. I have attended support groups only as an observer, not as a participant. I have read self-help books only as a critic, not as a seeker, and I was rarely engaged by the books that I read (one hundred or so), except as a critic. Whether this makes my analysis more or less worthwhile depends on whether you value the authority of experience more or less than the authority of research and reflection.

Writing on the basis of research and reflection, not experience, I'm writing counter to the Alcoholics Anonymous, twelve-step tradition currently in vogue. "Hi, I'm Wendy, and I'm a recovering alcoholic, overeater, drug abuser, shopper, or support group junkie," I'd be required to confess if I were writing a recovery book, offering advice. Instead I have only opinions and ideas; so although I imagine myself engaging in a dialogue with my readers, I don't imagine that we constitute a fellowship, based on shared experiences. Nor do I pretend to love my readers, any more than they love me and countless other strangers.

Perhaps because I have never trusted or desired protestations of affection or concern from strangers and mere acquaintances, I have never been attracted to support groups. It is often said that support groups offer community, and for people who attend the same group regularly and befriend other members that may well be true. But newcomers to meetings are considered part of the community too, so it is not necessarily based on friendship, if by friendship we mean bonds that build and strengthen over time. A twelve-step group seems a sad model for community. Testimony takes the place of conversation. Whether sitting in circles or lined up in rows, people take turns delivering monologues about themselves, rarely making eye contact with any of their listeners. Once, at an AA meeting I attended, a man testifying from the front row turned to look at us while he spoke, scanning our faces, seeking contact. Like everyone else I looked away; his behavior seemed inappropriate.

My own notion of intimacy does not include prurience — the exchange of secrets between strangers. My vision of community is shaped by an ideal of mutual respect between citizens and neighbors and a shared sense of courtesy and justice, but not love.

"Not all men are worthy of love," Freud wrote, debunking the religious ideal of unconditional love on which the recovery movement is based.[1] God loves us in spite of our flaws, as we must love each other, today's popular Protestant writers confirm. Or, as recovery experts might say, the love that discriminates, which Freud described, is a form of abuse. Like an Old Testament patriarch, Freud might be a model for an abusive, "shaming" parent.

Although the literature about recovery from addiction and codependency borrows heavily from family systems theory and seems, at first, an offshoot of pop psychology, it's rooted most deeply in religion. (Codependency is the disease from which everyone — alcoholics, drug abusers, shoppers, and sex addicts — is trying to recover.) The ideology of recovery is the ideology of salvation by grace. More than they resemble group therapy, twelve-step groups are like revival meetings, carrying on the pietistic tradition.

The religiosity of the recovery movement is evident in its rhetorical appeals to a higher power and in the evangelical fervor of its disciples. When I criticize the movement I am usually accused of being "in denial," as I might once have been accused of heresy. (There are only two states of being in the world of codependency — recovery and denial.) People who belong to twelve-step groups and identify strongly as addicts often turn on me with the self-righteous rage of religious zealots defending their gods.

Yet I have no power over them and want none. I'm not questioning their freedom to indulge in any religion or self-help movement. I'm not marketing a competing movement or exhorting them to do anything in particular with their lives. If they're happy in recovery, why do they resent and take personally the skepticism of strangers?

In fact, I don't intend my indictment of the recovery movement to be an indictment of every recovering person or even a comment on the movement's role in their lives. It is impossible to know how everyone in it uses this movement, interpreting or screening its messages to suit themselves. (It is equally impossible to know how many people are helped or hurt by individual therapy.) Countless people move in and out of support groups and read self-help books with varying degrees of attentiveness, skepticism, and naiveté. Some people say they've been helped by twelve-step groups, some say they've been hurt, and many have probably been affected indifferently.

This is not to minimize the popularity of the recovery movement, which, after all, is what makes it worth reviewing. Recovery gurus, such as John Bradshaw, have large and loyal followings; although sales of recovery and codependency books may have peaked, they are still in the millions. But, in the end, the testimonials of several million satisfied consumers are not exactly relevant to my critique. I'm not commenting on the disparate effects of the recovery movement or any other self-help program on the millions of individuals who partake in it. How could I? The individual effects of any mass movement are impossible to quantify. I'm commenting on the ideology of the recovery movement and its effect on our culture.

In questioning the collective impact of self-help trends, I'm making the unfashionable assumption, bound to irritate many, that it is still possible to talk about "our" culture in a self-consciously multicultural age. I'm assuming that Americans of different races, ethnicities, religions, genders, degrees of physical ablement, and socioeconomic classes may be affected by the same cultural phenomenon, such as television, celebrity journalism, confessional autobiographies, consumerism, and the preoccupation with addiction, abuse, and problem-solving techniques. Precisely how each group, tribe, or subculture is affected by these phenomena I leave to poststructural scholars to decide.

I'm not assuming, however, that self-help movements always represent every group of Americans they affect. Mainstream, mass market self-help books are generally written and published by whites and tend to target mostly white, broadly middle-class audiences. There are also, no doubt, historic racial divides in the self-help tradition, reflecting racial divides in society. My own reading of turn-of-the-century African-American self-improvement literature and conversations with African-

American scholars lead me to suspect that there is an African-American tradition oriented more toward communal, than individual, development; analogous self-improvement efforts among whites tended to emphasize the individual's progress up the ladder of success and salvation. Given the legacy of slavery and discrimination, it's not surprising that African-American self-help would focus more on "lifting the race." But diversity of opinion and ideals within racial and ethnic groups makes it difficult to label self-help movements distinctly black or distinctly white, the tradition of community activism and volunteering cuts across American culture, and the larger self-help tradition involving personal and communal development is a fairly pluralistic one. Early twentieth-century African-American leaders Marcus Garvey and Father Divine adopted some classic positive-thinking ideals — both were proponents of New Thought, a loose collection of beliefs about mind power that emerged in the nineteenth century. Today, Oprah Winfrey is a most effective proselytizer for recovery.

The divide in the self-help tradition that interests me is not demographic (racial, ethnic, sexual, or economic) but ideological: I'm distinguishing between practical (how to do your own taxes) books and personal (how to be happy) books. Of course, sometimes the practical and personal converge: Saving money on your taxes may make you a happy person. A diet book may offer helpful, practical advice on how to eat, while reinforcing cultural ideals of slimness and promising to boost your self-esteem. But if few books are purely personal or purely practical, some are clearly more personal. It is a strong emphasis on individual, personal, or spiritual development that connects the self-help ideals I'm reviewing and composes a tradition. It is that tradition I'm critiquing. How-to books may be appropriate guides to fixing your car, caring for your pet, or even organizing a political campaign. They are fundamentally in-apposite to resolving individual psychic or spiritual crises and forming an individual identity.

■   ■   ■

The self-help tradition has always been covertly authoritarian and conformist, relying as it does on a mystique of expertise, encouraging people to look outside themselves for standardized instructions on how to be, teaching us that different people with different problems can easily be saved by the same techniques. It is anathema to independent thought. Today's popular programs on recovery from various (and questionable) addictions actively discourage people from actually helping themselves. (Self-help is usually a misnomer for how-to programs in identity formation.) Codependency experts stress that people who shop or eat or love or drink too much cannot stop themselves by solitary exertions of will. Addiction is considered a disease of the will; believing in self-control is one of its symptoms.

That the self-help tradition is rarely described in these terms — as conformist, authoritarian, an exercise in majority rule — is partly a tribute to the power of naming. How could anything called self-help connote dependence? But the authoritarianism of this tradition is cloaked most effectively in the power of the marketplace to make it seem freely chosen. Choice is an American article of faith (as the vocabulary of the abortion debate shows; even antiabortion activists use the rhetoric of choice); and we exercise choice, or enjoy the illusion of it, primarily in the marketplace. We choose from myriad brands of tooth-paste and paper towels in the belief that they differ and reflect our own desires. We choose personal development experts, absorbing their maxims and techniques and making them our own.

With luck or good judgment, some readers find guides who are helpful or who at least will do no harm. The best self-help books are like good parents, dispensing common sense. Many more are like superfluous consultants, mystifying the obvious in jargon and italics to justify their jobs. "The first step in dismantling the kind of thinking that reinforces misery addiction is to identify what I call *miserable thoughts*," Robert A. Becker, Ph.D., announces in *Addicted to Misery*.[2] Experts package inanities as secrets that they're generously willing to divulge. In the best-selling *Secrets About Men Every Woman Should Know*, Beverly DeAngelis clears up such mysteries as "why men don't like to talk and have sex at the same time."[3] The answer, she says, simply restating her question, is that "men have a more difficult time expressing themselves and simultaneously performing a task than women do." What is the basis for this bold assertion about gender difference? There is only DeAngelis's claim to expertise — her Ph.D. and special insights into humankind. She is, after all, the author of *How to Make Love All the Time*.

This earnest fatuity that you find in self-help books is what makes them so funny. That millions of people take them seriously is rather sobering. We should be troubled by the fact that the typical mass market self-help book, consumed by many college-educated readers, is accessible to anyone with a decent eighth-grade education. We should worry about the willingness of so many to believe that the answers to existential questions can be encapsulated in the portentous pronouncements of bumper-sticker books. Only people who die very young learn all they really need to know in kindergarten.*

*Robert Fulghum's *All I Really Need to Know I Learned in Kindergarten* was the number one best-seller among college students for the 1989–1990 academic year. Fulghum was chosen as commencement speaker at Smith College in 1991 and offered an honorary degree, to the horror of at least a few alumnae.[4]

Some will call me an elitist for disdaining popular self-help literature and the popular recovery movement; but a concern for literacy and critical thinking is only democratic. The popularity of books comprising slogans, sound bites, and recipes for success is part of a larger, frequently bemoaned trend blamed on television and the failures of public education and blamed for political apathy. Intellectuals, right and left, complain about the debasement of public discourse the way fundamentalist preachers complain about sex. Still, to complain just a little — recently the fascination with self-help has made a significant contribution to the dumbing down of general interest books and begun changing the relationship between writers and readers; it is less collegial and collaborative than didactic. Today, even critical books about ideas are expected to be prescriptive, to conclude with simple, step-by-step solutions to whatever crisis they discuss. Reading itself is becoming a way out of thinking.

This book will not conclude with a ten- or twelve-point recovery plan for the "crisis of codependency," or the "codependency complex," or any other "self-help syndrome." If there is an easy way to get people to think for themselves, I haven't yet discovered it. (The hard way is education.) This book is not what publishers call prescriptive. As a writer and not a politician, I've always felt entitled to raise questions for which I have no answers, to offer instead a point of view.

ONE

Chances Are, You're Codependent Too: Recovery Books

Instead of a self-help section, my local bookstore has a section called recovery, right around the corner from the one called New Age. It's stocked with books about addiction, psychic healing, and codependency — the popular new disease blamed for such diverse disorders as drug abuse, alcoholism, anorexia, child abuse, compulsive gambling, chronic lateness, fear of intimacy, and low self-esteem. Codependence, which originally referred to the problems of women married to alcoholics, was discovered by pop psychologists and addiction counselors during the 1980s and redefined. Now it applies to any problem associated with any addiction, real or imagined, suffered by you or someone close to you. Now this amorphous disease is a business, generating millions of book sales, support groups, expensive treatment programs, and an annual recovery conference in Scottsdale, Arizona. Codependency "has arrived," according to the First National Conference Report issued in 1989; experts laud recovery as a national grass-roots movement.[1]

Codependency is advertised as a national epidemic, partly because every conceivable form of arguably compulsive behavior is classified as an addiction. We are a nation of sexaholics, rageholics, shopaholics, and rushaholics. What were once billed as bad habits and dilemmas — Cinderella and Peter Pan complexes, smart women loving too much and making foolish choices about men who hate them — are now considered addictions too, or reactions to the addictions of others, or both. Like drug and alcohol abuse, they are considered codependent diseases. If the self-help industry is any measure of our state of mind in the 1990s, we are indeed obsessed with disease and our capacity to defeat it. All codependency books stress the curative power of faith, introspection, and abstinence. It's morning after in America. We want to be in recovery.

Almost everyone — 96 percent of all Americans — suffers from codependency, experts assert, and given their very broad definitions of this disease, we probably do. Melody Beattie, best-selling author of *Codependent No More* and *Beyond Codependency*, defines codependency as being affected by someone else's behavior and obsessed with controlling it.[2] Who isn't? Anne Wilson Schaef, author of the best-selling *When Society Becomes an Addict* and *Co-Dependence: Misunderstood — Mistreated*, defines it as "a disease process whose assumptions, beliefs, and lack of spiritual awareness lead to a process of nonliving which is progressive."[3]

That some readers think they know what this means is a tribute to what George Orwell considered reduced expectations of language and the substitution of attitudes and feelings for ideas. It is enough for Schaef to mean that codependency is bad and anyone can have it, which makes this disease look more like a marketing device. Codependency offers a diagnosis, and support group, to virtually anyone with a problem who can read or listen to a tape cassette.

The publishing industry, which didn't exactly invent code-pendency, is making sure that millions of Americans discover it. Publishers ranging from HarperCollins to Prentice Hall to the religious press Thomas Nelson have special lines of recovery or wellness books. Harper San Francisco, a leader in the field, lists about eighty recovery books, some of which are published in conjunction with the Hazelden Foundation, a treatment center for chemical addiction. Sales can fairly be called phe-nomenal. Although publishers' sales figures are notoriously unreliable — they're likely to be inflated — there is no ques-tion that codependency books are extremely popular and profitable.

According to Harper's 1991 figures, one of its top sellers, Melody Beattie's *Codependent No More*, a paperback, has en-joyed over one hundred weeks on the *New York Times* best-seller list and sales of over two million. Beattie's *Beyond Codependency* has so far sold over 500,000 copies. Harper San Francisco also publishes Anne Wilson Schaef. Two of her books, *Co-Dependence: Misunderstood — Mistreated* and *Women's Real-ity: An Emerging Female System in a White Male Society*, have each sold over 300,000 copies. Her 1990 *Meditations for Women Who Do Too Much* has reportedly sold over 400,000 copies in one year.

Smaller publishers have also cashed in on this voracious market. Health Communications, Inc., which specializes in paperback codependency books, lists about two hundred titles, including some best-sellers. According to HCI's 1991 sales figures, its top book, *Adult Children of Alcoholics*, by Janet Woitetz, has sold over two million copies. Charles Whitfield's *Healing the Shame Within* and John Bradshaw's *Bradshaw On: The Family* and *Healing the Shame That Binds You* have each sold over 800,000 copies. HCI anticipates net sales of about two million for 1991.

What's striking about the innumerable codependency books on the market (I've read about thirty-five) is their sameness. They may differ in levels of literacy and how they balance discussion of codependency theory with recovery techniques. But they describe the same syndromes in the same jargon and prescribe the same cure — enlistment in a support group that follows an overtly religious program, stressing submission to a higher power, borrowed from Alcoholics Anonymous. Codependency books line the shelves like different brands of aspirin in a drugstore. As one codependency publisher has said, "A lot of people are looking at why they're not happy."[4]

Their unhappiness begins at home, in the dysfunctional family, codependency authors stress, drawing heavily on family systems theory explaining how individuals develop in relation or reaction to their families. In the world of codependency, families are incubators of disease: they manufacture "toxic" shame, "toxic" anger, "toxic" self-doubts, any number of "toxic" dependencies, and a "toxic" preoccupation with privacy. (Secrets are "toxic," presidential daughter Patti Davis confirms in *Vanity Fair*, explaining her decision to write a tell-all book about her parents, Ronald and Nancy Reagan.)

Codependency is blamed on bad parenting, or, put more dramatically, on child abuse, which makes it an intergenerational disease: child abuse — defined broadly to include any emotional or physical abandonment or disrespect — begets child abuse or anorexia and other forms of self-abuse. This is surely part of codependency's appeal. We are all fascinated by our families. No soap opera is more compelling than our own.

Codependency books lead you back through childhood to discover the many ways in which you've been abused and the "negative messages" you've internalized. Exercises, quizzes, and sentence completions, such as "I have trouble owning my feeling reality around my father when . . . ," assist you in self-evaluation and the obligatory "grief work." Discussion questions following each chapter test your reading comprehension. (Most of these books remind me of my grade school readers.) Meditations and visualizations help you work through your stopped-up energy systems. With simple diagnostic formulas you can estimate your codependency score, your place on a worry index, or your post-traumatic stress disorder (PTSD) average. You are encouraged to engage in "journaling," keeping track of your feelings on a daily basis. (Some codependency books, "workbooks," are filled with blank pages.) And you can find your own pattern or syndrome in the usual assortment of case studies that track pseudonymous and probably fictitious children of abuse into adulthood. Readers are encouraged to reconstruct their own pasts by drawing family trees ("genograms") charting their legacies of abuse: Grandfather was an alcoholic, mother is a compulsive rescuer, and Uncle Murray weighs 270 pounds. Father is a sex addict, your sister is anorexic, and you have affairs only with married men.

Encased in silliness and jargon may be some sensible insights into how character takes shape in the drama of family life. The trouble is that for codependency consumers, someone else is always writing the script. They are encouraged to see themselves as victims of family life rather than self-determining participants. They are encouraged to believe in the impossibility of individual autonomy; at least, codependency literature offers few lessons in the degrees of autonomy that people may achieve. The self is rarely viewed in isolation.

"We cannot have an identity all alone," John Bradshaw stresses in *Bradshaw On: The Family*, the 1988 best-seller based on his public television series. "Our reality is shaped from the beginning by a *relationship*."[5] I don't question the truth of this assertion, only its relative importance. Our reality is also shaped by the larger cultural environment — our race, religion, and socioeconomic status — as well as by the weather. Somewhere along the line we still become accountable for ourselves; the factors that shaped us are moot. If codependency authors make this point, it gets buried under a pile of family histories and relationship charts. The experts teach, with an air of discovery, that people are shaped by their families, as if family life always ended the story of character and never began it. For a self-help movement, recovery is remarkably deterministic.

The characters of children in dysfunctional families, which supposedly include virtually all families, are said to be determined early on by bad relationships: codependents are improperly "individuated." Codependents have boundary problems, confusion about where they end and others begin. "Growing up means accepting our fundamental aloneness," Bradshaw announces,[6] although no one is ever alone in recovery; outside your support group you're with God. But codependency authors are often inconsistent; sometimes, like politicians, they say what sounds right at the moment. Individuation is posited as a goal in recovery, but it's one that is hard to imagine achieving, given the premise that no one has an identity all alone. I suspect that improper individuation provides an excuse for recovering codependents more often than proper individuation provides a goal. Dysfunctional families sacrifice their members to the family system, Bradshaw assures us: *The individual exists to keep the system in balance.*[7]

In our culture, women have long been assigned primary responsibility for the family's emotional balance, and codependency is often described as a feminine disease, or femininity is labeled a form of codependency. Codependency is "women's basic programming," Charlotte Davis Kasl writes in *Women, Sex and Addiction*, a rare, reasonably intelligent, feminist analysis of addiction.[8] As pop New Age feminist Anne Wilson Schaef asserts in *Co-Dependence: Misunderstood — Mistreated*, "The non-liberated woman and the codependent are the same person. . . . She gets her identity completely from outside herself."[9] Many of the codependents described in codependency books are male, but most of these books are written for women — interested in their husbands and fathers as well as themselves. According to one publisher, the codependency market is 85 percent female.

There are differing feminist perspectives on this mostly female phenomenon. Stressing that women should not be submissive and self-effacing, the recovery movement includes some popular feminist ideals. But calling femininity a disease obscures the fact that many women are trapped in abuse by circumstance, not weakness. They enter into abusive marriages unwittingly, out of bad judgment or bad luck, not masochism; they remain because they can't afford to leave, perhaps because they've had less than equal educational or employment opportunities or because they have young children and no day care. Problems like these are political as well as personal; they require collective as well as individual action, and objectivity, as well as introspection.

But if the view of a nonliberated woman as sick is anathema to feminists who see her as oppressed, it's balanced by a view of liberation as healthy. Codependency theory harbors some soft feminist ideals, often couched in New Age jargon: John Bradshaw describes a good relationship as one "based on equality, the equality of two self-actualizing spiritual beings who connect at the level of their beingness."[10]

Whatever self-actualizing spiritual beings may be, however, there are few of them in this culture, male or female, Bradshaw and others agree: Women are not alone in their pathology. Men are sick in complementary ways, and society itself is addicted — to the arms race, the repression of emotion, the accumulation of capital, and enlarging the hole in the ozone layer. These addictions reflect what is implicitly condemned as the disease of masculinity — rationalist, "left-brain" thinking. As Anne Wilson Schaef asserts in *When Society Becomes an Addict*, the "White Male System" that rules us is addictive.[11] As she modestly reported in her earlier book, *Co-Dependence: Misunderstood — Mistreated*, "When we talk about the addictive process, we are talking about civilization as we know it."[12]

This view of codependency as a pervasive, institutionalized disease not only provides codependency authors with the widest possible audience — everyone — but imbues them with messianic zeal. Codependence, after all, is considered fatal, for individuals and the nation. It causes cancer and other stress-related diseases, experts warn, as well as environmental pollution and war.

If society and everyone in it is addicted, self-destructing, infected with left-brain rationality, then people in recovery are the chosen few, an elite minority of enlightened, if irrational, self-actualizers with the wisdom to save the world. Schaef confirms that the only people who can help cure our addictive system are those "recovering from its effects."[13]

Experts themselves must thus admit that they're recovering codependents too, and codependency books tend to be at least partly confessional, following a model of the expert as patient taken from AA: "Hello! My name is Carla and I am recovering from just about every addiction known to humanity," Carla Wills-Brandon perkily reveals on the first page of *Is It Love or Is It Sex?*[14] Personal experience with addiction is said to be as important a credential as professional degrees, partly because the therapeutic profession itself is said to be a nest of "practicing" codependents. Lynne Namka, author of *The Doormat Syndrome*, warns you to choose a therapist "who has fewer psychological problems than you do."[15]

These predictable confessions provide at most a fleeting appearance of an egalitarian relationship between expert and reader. One is still selling advice that the other is buying, and despite their pro forma identification with other recovering codependents, experts like to recite their professional credentials and carefully include any initials after their names: M.D.'s, M.A.'s, M.S.W.'s, and Ed.D.'s abound, joined by the occasional Ph.D. Experts who decline to cloak themselves in professional expertise, because they have none, invoke the moral authority we grant victims by confessing their addictions, as well as the respect we grant "survivors." In the 1990s, everyone wants to be a survivor, as if survivalhood were the only alternative to victimization: "QUAKE SURVIVOR RELOCATES seeks 'humanistic' male," a personal ad in the *New York Review of Books* explains. "I survived the subway strike, the summer of '88, my first husband," T-shirts proclaim. "I survived codependency," people in recovery may boast, like figures in a *New Yorker* cartoon cocktail party.

The process of recovery — it is not an event, experts repeatedly explain — may bring more than survival. The recovery "lifestyle" is supposed to bring rebirth. Its goal is healing your "inner child" — the wounded child who took refuge from deprivation and abuse in some recess of your soul.

Or perhaps the inner child is the soul: "*We all carry within us an eternal child,*" Jeremiah Abrams writes in *Reclaiming the Inner Child,* an eclectic collection of essays about the child within that are alternately engaging, trite, silly, and incomprehensible.[16] Inner child theory is an equally eclectic blend of Jung, New Age mysticism, holy child mythology, pop psychology, and psychoanalytic theories about narcissism and the creation of a false self that wears emotions without experiencing them.

Codependency, which includes narcissism, along with most other disorders, is often described as a failure to feel, or a failure to feel what's true: Addiction "masks" true feelings and the true childlike self. Codependents are considered "adult children." If some are more like Scrooge than Peter Pan, all have a Tiny Tim within.

Inner children are always good — innocent and pure — like the most sentimentalized Dickens characters, which means that people are essentially good and, most of all, redeemable: Even Ted Bundy had a child within. Evil is merely a mask — a dysfunction.

The therapeutic view of evil as sickness, not sin, is strong in codependency theory — it's not a fire and brimstone theology. "Shaming" children, calling them bad, is considered a primary form of abuse. Both guilt and shame "are not useful as a way of life," Melody Beattie writes earnestly in *Codependent No More*. "Guilt makes *everything* harder. . . . We need to forgive ourselves."[17] Someone should remind Beattie that there's a name for people who lack guilt and shame: sociopaths. We ought to be grateful if guilt makes things like murder and moral corruption "harder."

It's not quite fair, however, to accuse Beattie and other codependency experts of moral relativism, since they distinguish between healthy and unhealthy behavior. Outside a church or court of law the difference between sickness and sin may be merely semantic. Sickness, however, is more marketable than sin: readers who find it satisfying and useful to be diagnosed as the victims of disease would probably resent being called evil. Inner child doctrine assures us that no one is unforgivable; everyone can be saved. What looks at first like a therapeutic view of evil turns out to be religious instead: Codependency theory replaces the Freudian subconscious with its unholy impulses and dramas of inner conflict with the peaceful, happy vision of a child within. Because no one is inhabited by evil or "unhealthy" urges, because inside every addict is a holy child yearning to be free, recovery holds the promise of redemption.

This religiosity distinguishes codependency literature from the predominant personal development and relationship books of the 1970s and early 1980s. Prototypical books such as Colette Dowling's *The Cinderella Complex* and Dr. Joyce Brothers's *How to Get Whatever You Want Out of Life* focused on mental, not spiritual, health — on happiness, self-confidence, love, and success in the temporal world, not salvation. Codependency literature combines the pop psychology and pop feminism of these books with New Age spiritualism and, most of all, some traditional evangelical ideals. Addiction and recovery look a lot like sin and redemption. Addiction is often described as enthrallment to a false god; recovery leads you to the true. The suffering associated with addiction is purposeful and purifying, and it prepares you to serve: "Without my suffering, I would not be able to bear witness," John Bradshaw writes.[18] Sin can be the low road to redemption, as Jimmy Swaggart made clear. Many codependents take a familiar, confessional pride in their disorders, as if every addiction were a crucible.

It is not surprising that codependency theory has been embraced by a new generation of self-styled "Christian therapists." Thomas Nelson, the religious trade press, publishes a series of codependency books in conjunction with the Minirth-Meier clinic, a Christian psychiatric clinic in Texas. Instead of a generic higher power, the Minirth-Meier authors write about God and strongly suggest that everyone is better off with Jesus. They also tend to promote traditional sex roles and condemn feminism: abortion is a sin; mothers who become involved in political causes are engaging in abuse (the ways in which the very broad definitions of child abuse can be used against women become clear). But despite the overt Christian bias of these

books, they are, in substance, much like putatively secular codependency literature, using the same jargon to present the same
case studies, analyses of family life, and attitudes toward addiction. Because codependency theory is essentially religious and
essentially Christian as well, Christian therapists don't have
to adapt codependency; they simply adopt it.

The disease of codependency is probably millennium fever.
In this last decade of the twentieth century, everybody wants
to be reborn; and in recovery, everybody is. No matter how
bad you've been in the narcissistic 1970s and the acquisitive
1980s, no matter how many drugs you've ingested, or sex acts
performed, or how much corruption enjoyed, you're still essentially innocent: the divine child inside you is always untouched
by the worst of your sins.

■   ■   ■

This relentless optimism drove me to Kafka, that incorrigibly
unrepentant codependent, and to some old-fashioned preaching. God issues a lot of negative messages (thou shalt not's),
Rabbi Harlan J. Wechsler reminds us in *What's So Bad About
Guilt?*, a sensible, if avuncular, defense of conscience and rationality. Use your intellect to make moral judgments and devise
constructive punishments for yourself and others, he heretically
suggests: if your husband leaves you for a younger woman,
"berate him, punish him, and make his life miserable."[19]

Of course, there's no revenge in recovery, and little Old Testament justice. God issues only cloying positive messages — affirmations like "You are lovable." Chanting affirmations to yourself
daily is an important recovery technique. So is visualizing —
imagining yourself happy, spiritually "whole," or as your inner
child. "Energy follows thought," Lynne Namka reports in *The
Doormat Syndrome*. "You actually become what you think."[20]

"Picturize," Norman Vincent Peale commanded in *The Power of Positive Thinking*, back in 1952. If your husband wants to leave you, picture him sitting happily in his favorite chair, Peale suggested, and he'll stay. This is positively magical thinking, but, as Peale said, "what the mind profoundly expects, it tends to receive."[21] He advised readers to develop a "happiness habit" by repeating happy thoughts to themselves daily. Imagine yourself succeeding and you will, like The Little Engine That Could.

Codependency authors don't seem quite as materialistic or oblivious to social injustice as Peale (who believed all problems were failures of attitude), nor do they say recovery will be easy. But they owe him much — the reliance on simple, universally applicable techniques to facilitate individual change and the belief in automatic behavior, like the daily recitation of affirmations. The promise of a recovery "lifestyle" is that we need not remain victims of our families; the wounds of childhood need not be fatal. Codependency authors share with Peale the conviction that happiness, health, and spiritual well-being are available to everyone, requiring only faith and obedience to technique.

Recovery, after all, is not an act of will. Willfulness is what causes addiction; abdication, not continued assertion of the will, is its cure. ("I took back my will," I once heard a recovering alcoholic say, explaining a lapse back into drinking.) The first step in recovery is admitting that you are powerless over your addiction and incapable of willing your way to health; the next step is surrendering your will to a higher power. Demanding self-surrender, the recovery movement is essentially religious, not psychotherapeutic, and most closely resembles nineteenth-century revivalism, with a little Christian Science thrown in.

Imagine the slogan of recovery — admit that you're powerless and submit — as a political slogan, and what is wrong with this movement becomes clear. That is hardly a slogan for a participatory democracy. It is only a little less troubling as a slogan for a quasi-religious movement, particularly in light of the recent history of cultism in this country. I'm not suggesting that recovery is a cult (it's much too disorganized for that) or that recovery experts are all incipient Jim Joneses. A few do seem to enjoy the adulation of their followers and don't brook much dissent, but many are probably sincere, relatively benign advice givers. They stress that the mandate to submit is tempered by the fact that the concept of a higher power is presented as a very personal one: every man and woman gets to submit to his or her own image of God, which is no doubt better than submitting to somebody else's. But in fashioning a view of ourselves as passive or active, dependent or autonomous, how we imagine our gods may be less important than how we imagine our relationships with them — as submissive or collegial.

Recovery experts would also claim that the message about submission is not intended to absolve people from taking responsibility for their own recovery, and that is probably at least partly true. Getting over a genuine addiction or any destructive behavior pattern obviously requires individual motivation and self-discipline. It is also true that the religious ideals of self-surrender on which the recovery movement is based can be fairly complex, as numerous disputations about free will and salvation show.

Modern revivalism, which dates back to the early 1800s, was partly a revision of rather depressing and essentially un-American Calvinist notions about predestination and the inability of humankind to save itself. The first popular nineteenth-century revivalists, notably Charles Grandison Finney, rejected this notion that people are merely the passive recipients of grace or damnation: they can actively court salvation by opening their hearts to God and converting. Revivalism introduced ideas of human agency into the drama of salvation.[22]

But if every man and even woman had a role in the play, revivalist preachers, like Finney, were the stars. Itinerant preachers stumping the country facilitated conversions, purposefully exciting and manipulating people's emotions, drawing on their instincts about crowd psychology. God's salesmen, they knew how to advertise effectively. Finney even published a how-to book for aspiring preachers — a "professional handbook of revival techniques."[23]

Revivalism was a relatively egalitarian movement that bypassed established churches and focused on the individual's relationship with God. Recovery also is usually extolled for its egalitarianism; advocates claim that support groups provide no-cost, nonauthoritarian alternatives to traditional therapy, stressing that recovery, like salvation, is an individual journey. But it is not an autonomous one; it is not a journey you embark on alone. The irony of revivalism and recovery is that individual salvation is sought through submersion in a crowd.

Recovery hasn't quite given us back old-time religion; it offers a kinder, gentler, nonjudgmental god. Experts eschew stern and fearsome preaching; in their theology, denial is the closest you come to damnation. They often criticize overt, strict authoritarianism in church or in the home. Disapproving, rulebound parents breed "toxic" shame; disapproving, rulebound preachers breed "toxic" faith, as do New Age gurus, cult leaders, and other purveyors of "false" faiths. (Religion can be toxic too, the experts warn.) Codependency experts practice a very soft authoritarianism in their books, playing model parents for adult children to follow out of love and trust, not fear.

Like most modern ad campaigns, the recovery movement seems noncoercive. People aren't usually agitated or manipulated in obvious ways; the roles of the crowd and the expert are subtler than they are in revivalism. Consumers are free not to buy codependency books, and they determine their own degrees of participation in support groups, which are generally open to an anonymous public. No one is required to speak, and direct responses to anyone's testimony or comments on anyone else's problems are generally discouraged. The groups are supposed to be nonjudgmental, and you are supposed to talk only about yourself.

Yet, listening to recovering codependents describe their struggles in the same jargon and the same prefabricated phrases, you hear the voice of the crowd. Of course, speaking a common language is part of what holds a group together, and one measure of the success of any cultural phenomenon is the extent to which its language enters the vernacular. You knew the counterculture had peaked, for instance, when middle-aged, middle-class people started talking about the far-out things they were into. Today, people on line at the supermarket talk about their dysfunctional families.

Maybe it is possible to use someone else's jargon to convey your own thoughts. Maybe the jargon shapes the thought. But if the relationship between language and thought is a mystery, it's clear that recovering codependents not only use the same specialized language but often say the same things, partaking in the same popular attitudes toward addiction, abuse, and their own victimization.

I guess it is possible that their unanimity of opinion is evidence of its truth or, at least, its utility. "Why question what works?" I'm often asked. ("By their fruits ye shall know them.") A lot of people say they've found the answers in recovery, as well as support, self-esteem, and what experts might call a lifestyle system. "It saved my life," some declare in dramatic defense of recovery, and if that's true I'm happy for them.

But without questioning their right to choose their gateways to salvation, I can question their judgment as well as prevailing claims about the general efficacy of twelve-step groups. No one really knows just how well recovery works. People who are helped by twelve-step groups may have been helped by other treatments and sets of beliefs, and the actual success or failure rates of disease model treatment programs, like AA, have been credibly questioned by other "experts in the field."[24] But you don't have to be a therapist, M.D., or any other certifiable expert in drug or alcohol abuse and other bad behaviors to wonder about a society in which people are so eager to call themselves addicted and abused.

Whether alcoholism is an inheritable disease or a learned behavior is a controversy about which I have no opinion. (I do doubt, however, that absolutely everyone who drinks habitually or in excess is the victim of her genes.) Some drugs are indisputably addictive, and the Narcotics Anonymous meetings I've attended clarified for me the uses of support. (What I've occasionally heard recovering addicts describe is support that includes some active intervention.) Smoking may be addictive for some people, but many have given up cigarettes by exertions of will, without the aid of any program. Some people eat, shop, have sex, or twirl their hair compulsively, but I doubt it's helpful to convince them that they're powerless to stop. Practicing overeaters, shoppers, and twirlers, like drugs addicts, are even warned against trying to stop eating, shopping, or twirling on their own: a belief in self-control is a symptom of codependency and the "perfectionist complex." Exaggerating every foible, bad habit, and complaint, taking our behavior out of our control, and defining us as adult children, recovery encourages invalidism. Calling the recovery process self-help doesn't change the way it tends to disempower people.

It is an odd program in self-esteem that rewards people for calling themselves helpless, childish, addicted, and diseased and punishes them for claiming to be healthy. Admit that you're sick and you're welcomed into the recovering persons fold; dispute it and you're "in denial." Thus the search for identity is perversely resolved: all your bad behaviors and unwanted feelings become conditions of your being. Instead of a person who smokes, you are a nicotine addict. Instead of a person who is sometimes depressed, you are a sadness addict. (Feelings can be addictive too, we're told.)

The popularity of these diagnoses reflects, in part, a natural preference for a treatable disease — codependency — over the undefinable sense of unease from which everyone must sometimes suffer. Codependency experts stress that *disease* is *"disease,"* with the ersatz profundity of adolescents discovering that *God* is *dog* spelled backward; but unlike the adolescents, the experts miss their point. Identifying codependency with what some might consider the human condition only undercuts the claim that it is a discrete dysfunction from which people may recover.

Labeling all their problems symptoms of disease, people in recovery find not only the promise of a cure but an external cause for what ails them — the dysfunctional family (and their families in particular). Codependency experts assert that practically everyone is a victim of child abuse, defining abuse broadly enough to make the assertion true. Who among us has ever enjoyed or could ever provide always perfect parenting?

The unwillingness to tolerate, much less laugh at, the inevitable conflicts and imperfections of family life may be poignant in adolescents, but it is tiresome in adults. It also impedes efforts to address serious patterns of abuse. When the minor mistakes that every parent makes are dramatized, or melodramatized, the terrible misconduct of some is trivialized. If child abuse is every form of inadequate nurturance, then being raped by your father is in the same general class as being ignored or not getting help with your homework. When everything is child abuse, nothing is.

There is something niggardly and mean-spirited in the passion with which some recovering codependents point to themselves as victims of abuse, laying claim to the crown of thorns. Adult Children of Alcoholics (ACOAs) are like Holocaust survivors, suffering post-traumatic stress disorder, John Bradshaw writes offensively.[25] Recovery gives people permission always to put themselves first, partly because it doesn't give them a sense of perspective on their complaints: parental nagging is not the equal of physical abuse and deprivation, much less genocide; vague intimations of unease are not the same as cancer. No one seems to count her blessings in recovery. I've heard no one say, "Some people suffer more than I." For all the talk about sharing and caring, in recovery there's more evidence of self-pity than compassion.

The failure to acknowledge that there are hierarchies of human suffering is what makes recovery and other personal development fashions "selfist" and narcissistic, as critics charge. That is not, however, a failure of individualism. Thinking for yourself and considering your existential autonomy does not mean losing your sense of place in society and the understanding that other people's problems may be more pressing than your own. The selfism of recovery is more a failure of community; at least it reflects a very shallow notion of community, which is not a group of people going on about themselves in the belief that they're all equal in their pain. Community requires an awareness of inequalities, the desire to correct them, and faith in your capacity to do so — faith that the human will can sometimes be a force for good, not just the blackened, shriveled heart of a disease. *"The will is the most dis-eased part of any adult child's co-dependence,*" Bradshaw writes,[26] and since practically everyone is supposed to be an adult child, practically everyone must surrender the will in order to recover, which doesn't leave us with many possibilities for willful, moral actions. That recovery is extolled by its advocates as a paradigm of community and condemned by critics for excessive individualism only measures our confusion about individualism and community. It also reflects a pervasive fascination with victimhood as a primary source of identity. Acted upon, put upon, and always aggrieved, adult children, the victims of their families, are hardly models for individual or communal action. Yet this emphasis on the essential helplessness of the individual has perverse appeal. It offers absolution and no accountability, and instead of imposing the capacity to act, it confers entitlements to sympathy, support, and reparations.

The phenomenal success of the recovery movement reflects two simple truths that emerge in adolescence: all people love to talk about themselves, and most people are mad at their parents. You don't have to be in denial to doubt that truths like these will set us free.

TWO

Testifying: Television

Recovering substance abuser Kitty Dukakis once called a press conference to announce her descent into alcoholism and request respect for her privacy. It was shortly after her husband's defeat in the 1988 presidential race, when she was less newsworthy than the pearls adorning Barbara Bush's neck. I marveled only briefly at the spectacle of a woman seeking privacy in a press conference and public confession of an addiction. Some people, especially famous and formerly famous ones, seem to enjoy their privacy only in public. *Now You Know*, Kitty Dukakis called her book, in case you cared.

Still, millions of readers who don't care about Dukakis and all the other recovering personalities who write books are curious, I guess. Confessional autobiographies by second-string celebrities are publishing staples (and where would the talk shows be without them?) Ali MacGraw exposes her sex addiction and the lurid details of her marriage to Steve McQueen. Suzanne Somers chronicles her life as an ACOA. Former first children Michael Reagan and Patti Davis reveal their histories of abuse.

"I truly hope my book will help others to heal," the celebrity diarists are likely to say. Or they assure us that writing their books was therapeutic (and if they pay me to read them, I will). But the celebrities don't really have to explain the decision to go public. In our culture of recovery we take their confessions for granted. Talking about yourself is "part of the process." Suggesting to someone that she is talking too much about herself is a form of abuse. If you can't feign interest in someone else's story, you're supposed to maintain respectful or, better yet, stunned silence. In recovery, where everyone gets to claim that she's survived some holocaust of family life, everyone gets to testify.

The tradition of testifying in court, church, or the marketplace for justice, God, or the public good is a venerable one that I would not impugn. But it is also a tradition I'd rather not debase by confusing testifying with advertisements for yourself or simple plays for sympathy and attention. The recovery movement combines the testimonial tradition that serves a greater good, like justice, with the therapeutic tradition in which talking about yourself is its own reward. It also borrows liberally from the revivalist tradition of testifying to save your soul and maybe others: in recovery, even the most trivial testimony is sanctified.

I'm not impugning therapy or religion either, but I wish that people would keep them off the streets. Religion has, of course, a complicated, controversial history of public uses and abuses, which are beyond the scope of this book. But therapy was conceived as a private transaction between doctors and patients (experts and clients) or between groups of patients, clients, seekers of psychic well-being. Testimony was public. By blurring the distinction between confession and testimony, recovery transforms therapy into a public process too. People even do it on TV.

Most of us do love to talk about ourselves, although I've always regarded it as a slightly illicit pleasure or one you pay for by the hour. Etiquette books dating back over a century gently admonish readers to cultivate the art of listening, assuming that, unmannered in their natural states, most people are braggarts and bores. Success primers have always stressed that listening skills will help you get ahead: Listen raptly to someone in power who loves talking about himself in order to impress him with your perspicacity. Listening is a useful form of flattery, Dale Carnegie advised, sharing with men what women have always known. Flirting is a way of listening. (Feminism is women talking.)

For women who were socialized to listen, uncritically, talking too much about themselves may feel like an act of rebellion. Maybe Kitty Dukakis felt liberated by her book. Personal development passes for politics, and what might once have been called whining is now exalted as a process of asserting selfhood; self-absorption is regarded as a form of self-expression, as if creative acts involved no interactions with the world. Feminists did say that the personal was political, but they meant that private relations between the sexes reflected public divisions of power, that putatively private events, like wife beating, were public concerns. They didn't mean that getting to know yourself was sufficient political action. Consciousness raising was supposed to inspire activism. Feminism is women talking, but it is not women only talking and not women talking only about themselves.

Talk shows and the elevation of gossip to intellectual discourse are, after all, postfeminist, postmodern phenomena. In academia, where gossip is now text, poststructural scholars scour history for the private, particular experiences of ordinary "unempowered" people; and like denizens of daytime TV, they also talk a lot about themselves, deconstructing their own class, racial, or ethnic biases in perverse assertions of solidarity with what are presumed to be other entirely subjective selves. On talk shows, ordinary people, subject of tomorrow's scholars, find their voice. Men and mostly women distinguished only by various and weird infidelities or histories of drug abuse and overeating get equal time with movie actors, soap stars, and the occasional hair stylist. Now everyone can hope for sixty minutes of fame, minus some time for commercials.

I never really wonder anymore why people want to talk about themselves for nearly an hour in front of millions of strangers. They find it "affirming"; like trees that fall in the forest, they're not sure that they exist when no one's watching. I've accepted that as postmodern human nature. I do wonder at the eagerness and pride with which they reveal, on national television, what I can't help thinking of as intimacies — sexual and digestive disorders; personal conflicts with parents, children, spouses, lovers, bosses, and best friends. I wonder even more at the intensity with which the audience listens.

Why aren't they bored? It may be that listening is simply the price they pay for their turn to grab the mike and have their say, offering criticism or advice, just like the experts. But they seem genuinely intrigued by the essentially unremarkable details of other people's lives and other people's feelings. Something in us likes soap operas, I know, but watching the talks is not like watching "Dallas" or "Days of Our Lives." The guests aren't particularly articulate, except on "Geraldo" sometimes, where they seem to be well coached; they rarely finish their sentences, which trail off in vague colloquialisms, you know what I mean? Most guests aren't witty or perceptive or even telegenic. They aren't artful. They are the people you'd ignore if you saw them on line at the supermarket instead of on TV.

I'm not sure how we got to the point of finding anyone else's confessions, obsessions, or advertisements for herself entertaining. I'm not sure why watching other people's home movies became fun; the appeal of "America's Funniest Home Videos" eludes me. But it's clear that the popularity of "real people" television — talk shows and home videos — has little to do with compassion and the desire to connect. If an average person on the subway turns to you, like the ancient mariner, and starts telling you her tale, you turn away or nod and hope she stops, not just because you fear she might be crazy. If she tells her tale on camera, you might listen. Watching strangers on television, even responding to them from a studio audience, we're disengaged — voyeurs collaborating with exhibitionists in rituals of sham community. Never have so many known so much about people for whom they cared so little.

■   ■   ■

A woman appears on "Oprah Winfrey" to tell the nation that she hates herself for being ugly. Oprah and the expert talk to her about self-esteem and the woman basks, I think, in their attention. The spectacle is painful and pathetic, and watching it, I feel diminished.

Oprah, I suspect, regards her show as a kind of public service. The self-proclaimed ugly woman is appearing on a segment about our obsession with good looks. We live in a society that values pretty people over plain, Oprah explains; and maybe she is exploring a legitimate public issue, by exploiting a private pathology.

Daytime TV, however, is proudly pathological. On "Geraldo" a recovering sex addict shares a story of incest — she was raped by her father and stepfather; her husband and children are seated next to her on the stage. This is family therapy. (The family that reveals together congeals together.) Her daughter talks about being a lesbian. Two sex addiction experts — a man and a woman, "professional and personal partners" — explain and offer commentary on sex and love addictions. "It's not a matter of frequency," they say in response to questions about how often sex addicts have sex. Anonymous addicts call in with their own tales, boring and lurid: "I do specifically use sex to make myself feel better," one caller confesses. Who doesn't?

Geraldo, his experts, and the members of his audience address the problem of promiscuity with the gravity of network anchors discussing a sub-Saharan famine. If I were a recovering person, I might say that they're addicted to melodrama. In fact, Geraldo does a show on people "addicted to excitement — drama, danger, and self-destruction" — people who create crises for themselves. He offers us a self-evaluation tool — eleven questions "to determine whether you're a soap opera queen." Do you get mad at other drivers on the road? Do you talk about your problems with a lot of other people? Questions like these make addicts of us all, as experts must hope. Labeling impatience in traffic a symptom of disease creates a market for the cure; and Joy Davidson, the expert/author who identified the "soap opera syndrome" for us is here on "Geraldo," peddling her book.

The audience is intrigued. People stand up to testify to their own experiences with drama and excitement addictions. With the concern of any patient describing her symptoms, one woman says that she often disagrees with her husband for no good reason. Someone else confesses to being a worrier.

No one suggests to Davidson that calling the mundane concerns and frustrations of daily life symptoms of the disease of overdramatizing is, well, overdramatizing. In the language of recovery, we might say that Davidson is an enabler, encouraging her readers to indulge in their melodrama addictions, or we might say that she too is a practicing melodrama addict. One man does point out that there are "people in the ghetto" who don't have to fabricate their crises. But if Davidson gets the point, she successfully eludes it. Yes, she admits, the crises in the ghetto are real, but what matters is the way you deal with them. As Norman Vincent Peale might say, people in crisis have only to develop a happiness habit.

Meanwhile, on daytime TV, middle-class Americans are busy practicing their worry habits, swapping stories of disease and controversial eccentricities. Here is a sampling of "Oprah": Apart from the usual assortment of guests who eat, drink, shop, worry, or have sex too much, there are fathers who sleep with their sons' girlfriends (or try to), sisters who sleep with their sisters' boyfriends, women who sleep with their best friends' sons, women who sleep with their husbands' bosses (to help their husbands get ahead), men who hire only pretty women, and men and women who date only interracially. Estranged couples share their grievances while an expert provides on-air counseling: "Why are you so afraid to let your anger out at her?" he asks a husband. "Why don't you let him speak for himself," he chides the wife. Couples glare at each other, sometimes the women cry, and the expert keeps advising them to get in touch with their feelings and build up their self-esteem. The chance to sit in on someone else's therapy session is part of the appeal of daytime TV. When Donahue interviews the children of prostitutes, he has an expert on hand to tell them how they feel.

The number of viewers who are helped by these shows is impossible to know, but it's clear that they're a boon to several industries — publishing, therapy, and, of course, recovery. Commercials often tie in to the shows. A segment on food addiction is sponsored by weight-loss programs: "It's not what you're eating. It's what's eating you," the ads assure anxious overeaters. Shows on drug and alcohol abuse are sponsored by treatment centers, set in sylvan glades. Standing by lakes, leaning on trees, the pitchmen are soft and just a little somber — elegaic; they might be selling funeral plots instead of a recovery lifestyle and enhanced self-esteem.

On almost every show, someone is bound to get around to self-esteem; most forms of misconduct are said to be indicative of low self-esteem. On every other show, someone talks about addiction. The audiences usually speak fluent recovery. You can talk about your inner child or your grief work on "Oprah" and no one will ask you what you mean. "I follow a twelve-step program that helps me deal with the disease concept, the addiction [to overeating]," a man in the audience announces, and people nod. No one asks, "What's a twelve-step program?" or "What do you mean by addiction?" Oprah testifies too: "I'm still addicted [to food]. I'll never be free."

Onstage, a panel of recovering food addicts, all women, is vowing never to diet again. "We have to allow ourselves to love ourselves," they say, and Oprah agrees. "I'm never going to weigh another piece of chicken." Tired of "seeking control," these women want to accept their weight, not constantly struggle to lose it, and I wish them luck. Beauty may lack moral value, but it's useful, and what has been labeled beastly — obesity or really bad skin — is a painful liability, as the women on "Oprah" make clear. They've apparently spent much of their lives embarrassed by their bodies; now, in recovery, they talk about the "shame" of fatness. They find some self-esteem in victimhood. They aren't gluttons but "victims of a disease process." Being fat is not their fault. Recovering from obesity "is not about self-control," one woman says, voicing the ethos of recovery that dispenses with will. "It's about self-love."

But the next day, when Oprah does a show on troubled marriages, some sort of therapist, Dr. Ron, advises a woman who is self-conscious about her small breasts to have implants. He berates her unfaithful husband for not supporting her in this quest for a better body, for her own good, for the sake of her self-esteem, and to help save their marriage: her poor self-image was one of the reasons he strayed. That a woman with small breasts can't be expected to improve her self-esteem without implants is apparently evident to Dr. Ron and everyone else on the show. No one questions his wisdom, not even learning-to-love-herself Oprah, recovering dieter.

I digress, but so do Geraldo, Donahue, and Oprah. Talking about these shows, I find it hard to be entirely coherent, and coherence would not do justice to the kaleidoscope of complaints, opinions, prejudices, revelations, and celebrations they comprise: Geraldo discusses celibacy with a panel of virgins and Helen Gurley Brown. "There are no medical risks associated with virginity," a doctor assures us. Adopted children and their biological parents as well as siblings separated from birth for over twenty years meet, for the first time, on "Geraldo" ("Reunions of the Heart: Finding a Lost Love," the show is called). "Welcome long-lost brother Brian," Geraldo commands, to wild applause, as Brian emerges from backstage, and in a TV minute people are hugging and sobbing on camera as they did years ago in "This Is Your Life." I want someone in the audience to ask them why they're not having their reunions in private, but I already know the answer. "We want to share the love and joy of this moment," they'd say. "We want to inspire other people from broken families not to give up the search." I suspect that the audience knows these answers too. Clapping and crying (even Geraldo is teary), reached for and touched, they offer support and validation: "It's a real blessing to see how you've all been healed of your hurts," one woman in the audience declares. Geraldo makes a plea for open adoption, grappling with an issue, I guess.

Occasionally, I admit, the shows are instructive in ways they intend, not just as portraits of popular culture. Donahue's segment on grandparents who are raising the children of their drug-addicted children manages to be dignified and sad. He talks to obese children without overdramatizing their struggles or exploiting them. (Donahue is good with kids.) Oprah seems likable and shrewd in the midst of her silliest shows, and, once in a while, the testimony illuminates an issue: date rape or racially segregated proms.

This is the new journalism — issues packaged in anecdotes that may or may not be true. As an occasional, alternative approach to news and analysis, it is affecting; as the predominant approach, it is not just trite but stupefying. If all issues are personalized, we lose our capacity to entertain ideas, to generalize from our own or someone else's experiences, to think abstractly. We substitute sentimentality for thought.

TV talk shows certainly didn't invent the new journalism and are hardly the only abusers of it. But they are emblematic of the widespread preference for feelings over ideas that is celebrated by recovery and other personal development movements. It is no coincidence that the two trends — talk shows and recovery — have fueled each other. The shows often seem like orchestrated support groups; the groups seem like rehearsals for the shows.

Accusing talk shows of not providing critical analysis of issues is, I know, like accusing "Ozzie and Harriet" of idealizing the nuclear family. "He wrestles with the obvious," a friend once said of an especially boring pundit, and I don't mean to wrestle with TV. I just wanna testify too.

■   ■   ■

Once, I appeared on the "Oprah Winfrey" show. I was one of six alleged experts participating in what was billed as a "debate" on codependency. Joining me onstage were two against-codependency allies and three for-codependency opponents. (The two sides were driven in separate limousines and kept in separate rooms before the show.) Oprah was more or less pro-codependency too — someone said she had just returned from one of John Bradshaw's retreats — and the audience seemed filled with evangelical twelve steppers.

"Just jump in. Don't wait to be called on," one of Oprah's people told us when she prepped us for the show. "You mean you want us to interrupt each other?" I asked; the woman nodded. "You want us to be really rude and step on each other's lines?" She nodded again. "You want us to act as if we're at a large, unruly family dinner on Thanksgiving?" She smiled and said, "You got it!"

I had a good time on "Oprah." Being chauffeured around in a limo and housed in a first-class hotel, I felt like Cinderella, especially when I got home. I liked being on national television, almost as much as my mother liked watching me. I also like unruly family dinners, but I'd never call what goes on over the turkey a debate.

The trouble with talk shows is that they claim to do so much more than entertain; they claim to inform and explain. They dominate the mass marketplace and help make it one that is inimical to ideas.

That's probably not a startling revelation, but appearing on a talk show, you are hit hard with the truth of it. Being on "Oprah" was still a shock, although not a surprise. I watch a fair amount of talk shows and understand the importance of speaking in sound bites, although I don't always succeed in doing so. I know that talk show "debates" are not usually coherent; they don't usually follow any pattern of statement and response. They don't make sense. The host is less a moderator than a traffic cop. People don't talk to each other; they don't even talk at each other. They talk at the camera. So I wasn't surprised when Oprah's assistant told us to "just jump in." I expected the show to be chaotic (the experience exceeded the expectation). What I did not expect, and should have, was the audience's utter lack of interest in argument; they wanted only to exchange testimony.

I had nothing to say to the studio audience — and talked at the camera too — because I had no personal experience with addiction and recovery to convey. The most popular "expert" on our panel was the most melodramatic: Lois, a recovering codependent from Texas, declared repeatedly, in response to nothing in particular, "Mah parents died of this disease!" ("What disease?" we asked, in vain.) "Recovery saved mah life!" Once or twice she added cryptically, "Ah was not supposed to be born! Ah was a mistake!" as the audience applauded.

On daytime talk shows a "debate" generally consists of a parade of people onstage or in the audience stating strong personal preferences with frequent references to some searing personal experience. "Does too!" "Does not!" people say, debating whether the recovery movement helps us. "I'm a recovering person and I just want to say that this movement saved my life," members of the audience on "Oprah" declared. "I would be dead today if it weren't for this movement!"

You can't argue with a testimonial. You can only counter it with a testimonial of your own. ("Does too!" "Does not!") Testimony has no value as argument. You can't even be sure of its value as testimony. Is it true? What do people mean when they say that they are addicted? Addicted to what, at what cost? What do people mean when they say they've been abused? Are they talking about emotional or physical abuse? Was it real or imagined? Were they beaten by their parents or ignored? "What are you all recovering from?" one man in the back row of Oprah's audience asked repeatedly and in vain as self-proclaimed recovering persons testified.

But if you can't evaluate or argue with testimony, you can say that it's beside the point. How one hundred people in a studio audience feel about codependency doesn't tell us very much about its impact on the culture, or even its general success and failure rate with individuals. Testimony often precludes analysis. What was striking to me about the audience on "Oprah" was its collective inability or unwillingness to think about recovery in any terms other than the way it made them feel. To the extent that they commented on it as a cultural phenomenon at all, they simply universalized their own experiences: "It worked for me. So it will work for everyone else."

Testifying, as a substitute for thinking, is contagious. You even find it in the halls of academe. Teaching college freshmen, I quickly discovered that my students were interested only in issues that were dramatized — in fiction, memoirs, or popular journalism. Raised on "Donahue" and docudramas, they found mere discussions of ideas "too dry and academic." You can't even be academic in academia anymore. Instead of theory, they sought testimony.

Among graduate students and professors too, subjectivity has been in fashion for several years. The diversification of student populations and concern for multiculturalism have made respect for subjective experiences and points of view political imperatives. Fashions in literary and legal theory and historical research focus on knowledge as a matter of perspective, disdaining the "pretense" of objectivity. Scholars get to talk about themselves. Theory is nothing but testimony.

I'm not suggesting that the dead white males who once held sway and set standards had The Answer or that a multiplicity of perspectives in matters of politics and theory isn't welcome. Nor am I suggesting that analysis should somehow be divorced from experience. I'm only suggesting the obvious — that analysis and experience need to be balanced. There are degrees of objectivity worth trying to acquire.

It should be needless to say that individual preferences are not always the best measures of what is generally good. A tax provision that saves you money may still be generally unfair. Of course, the recovery movement is not analogous to the tax code. It is not imposed on us. It is not a public policy that demands deliberation and debate. I don't want to gloss over the difference between public acts and private experiments with personality development. Indeed, I want to highlight it.

A self-referential evaluation of a self-help movement is probably inevitable and, to some extent, appropriate. A self-referential evaluation of public policies can be disastrous. What is disturbing about watching the talk shows is recognizing in discussions of private problems a solipsism that carries over into discussions of public issues. What you see on "Oprah" is what you see in the political arena. We choose our elected officials and formulate policies on the basis of how they make us feel about ourselves. (Jimmy Carter's biggest mistake was in depressing us.) We even evaluate wars according to their effect on our self-esteem: Vietnam was a downer. The Persian Gulf War, like a good self-help program, cured us of our "Vietnam syndrome" and "gave us back our pride," as General Motors hopes to do with Chevrolets. Norman Schwarzkopf and Colin Powell satisfied our need for heroes, everyone said. The networks stroked us with video montages of handsome young soldiers, leaning on tanks, staring off into the desert, wanting to "get the job done" and go home. By conservative estimates, 150,000 people were killed outright in the war; the number who will die from disease, deprivation, and environmental damage may be incalculable. Whether or not the war was necessary, whether or not the victory was real, we shouldn't consider it a great success because it gave us parades and a proud Fourth of July. The culture of recovery is insidious: now the moral measure of a war is how it makes us feel about ourselves.

"Try and put aside your own experiences in recovery and the way it makes you feel," I suggested to the audience on "Oprah." "Think about what the fascination with addiction means to us as a culture. Think about the political implications of advising people to surrender their will and submit to a higher power." People in the audience looked at me blankly. Later, in the limo, one of my copanelists (against codependency) shook his head at me and smiled and said, "That was a PBS comment."

Some two months later I showed my "Oprah" tape to a group of college friends, over a bottle of wine. None of them is involved in the recovery movement or familiar with its programs or jargon. Listening to six panelists and a studio audience compete for air time, in eight-minute segments between commercials, none of them thought the "Oprah" show made any sense. Like the man in the audience who asked, "What are you all recovering from?" they didn't have a clue. "You have to think with your hearts and not your heads," a for-codependency expert exhorted us at the end of the show, as the credits rolled.

THREE

Don't Worry, Be
Happy: Positive
Thinking to est

For more than two hundred years self-help experts have been discovering the secret to wealth, health, and spiritual well-being, for the first time: America's fascination with self-help is older than the republic itself. In the colonies, Puritan self-improvement literature told readers how to lead godly, Protestant lives. Soon Ben Franklin was telling them how to succeed in the secular sphere. In the 1800s, books on etiquette, femininity, homemaking, sexual purity, and success guided men and women through an increasingly complicated, industrialized world. Popular fiction was equally didactic: the prominent nineteenth-century women's magazine *Godey's Lady's Book* offered moral tales on female virtue and family life. Both sexes sought spiritual guidance. Before New Age there was New Thought, an amorphous collection of beliefs about the power of mind and spirit to transcend mere material realities (and generate wealth). Before Norman Vincent Peale, Werner Erhard, and Shirley MacLaine there were Mary Baker Eddy, founder of Christian Science, and Napoleon Hill, hopeful author of *Think and Grow Rich*.

In the self-help universe, anything is possible: anyone can be rich, thin, healthy, and spiritually centered with faith, discipline, and the willingness to take direction. This pragmatic optimism is supposed to be singularly American, and we tend to be as proud of the self-help tradition as we are enamored of the notion that we are a country of people forever inventing ourselves.

The how-to phenomenon does reflect a democratic belief in the individual's capacity to overcome circumstances of nature and class — but only through adherence to systems that are devised or discovered by experts. The recovery movement is only the latest in a line of personal developments that encourage surrender of will, to a system if not a higher power, and unqualified acceptance of an expert's advice. If the self-help tradition acknowledges some democratic ideals, it also undermines them by encouraging people not to think for themselves or to question the possibility of panaceas. The potentially dangerous gullibility of many self-help consumers is demonstrated by the sheer silliness of the most popular and historically resilient self-help ideal — positive thinking.

"The happiness habit is developed simply by practicing happy thinking," Norman Vincent Peale assured America in 1952 in *The Power of Positive Thinking*, which sold millions of copies and, forty years later, remains in print. Peale declared that the greatest problem facing Americans was "lack of self-confidence" (expert revelations about self-esteem are hardly new). Peale conceded that "there may be such a thing as the 'bad breaks' in this life," but he doesn't really believe in them, any more than he admitted the possibility of social injustice.[1]

Thus the secret to success is simply believing you'll succeed and putting faith in Jesus. How do you shed your doubts and become one of the faithful? The "ultimate method for having faith is simply to *have faith,*" Peale announced in an earlier book, *Faith Is the Answer.*[2] What is the "scientific" technique for becoming a happy, prosperous person? Make a list of happy thoughts and replay them to yourself daily. "While dressing or shaving or getting breakfast say aloud a few remarks such as the following, 'I believe this is going to be a wonderful day.'" That is "affirmation therapy" or "the technique of suggestive articulation," repeating aloud "some peaceful words. Words have profound suggestive power," Peale confirms. Simply saying the word *tranquillity* "tends to induce a tranquil state."[3]

What is most striking about Peale's secret, scientific techniques is that they are not techniques at all, any more than they are secret or scientific. They are simply maxims and commands: Happy thoughts ensure a happy life. Pray, or "prayerize," and "picturize." Imagine what you want and it will come to you. Most of all, don't worry.

Avoid "worry conversations," Peale advised. "It is important to eliminate from conversations all negative ideas, for they tend to produce tension and annoyance inwardly. . . . reduce the number of worry words in your conversation. . . . [worry] is simply an unhealthy and destructive mental habit."[4] To suggest that some personal, political, or social problems might be worth worrying about misses Peale's point: the mother of all problems is a negative state of mind. To call Peale's philosophy mindless is only to praise it: an empty mind is a receptacle for faith.

"I recommend emptying the mind at least twice a day," he writes. "Definitely practice emptying your mind of fears, hates, insecurities, regrets, and guilt feelings." He calls this a "process of mind drainage. . . . fear thoughts, unless drained off, can clog the mind and impede the flow of mental and spiritual power."[5] Today we tend to imagine the brain as a computer, actively processing information; Peale thought of it as the kitchen sink, with God as the plumber:

> Picture all the worry thoughts flowing out of you as you would let water flow from a basin by removing the stopper. Repeat the following affirmation during this visualization: "With God's help I am now emptying my mind of all anxiety, all fear, all sense of insecurity." Repeat this slowly five times, then add, " I believe that my mind is now emptied of all anxiety, all fear, all sense of insecurity." Repeat that statement five times, meanwhile holding a mental picture of your mind as being emptied of these concepts. Then thank God for thus freeing you from fear. Then go to sleep.[6]

Once, with God's help, you have emptied your head, it is ready to be filled with faith:

> Say aloud such affirmations as the following: "God is now filling my mind with courage, with peace, with calm assurance. God is now protecting me from all harm. God is now protecting my loved ones from all harm. God is now guiding me to right decisions. God will see me through this situation."[7]

Peale indulged in some rhetoric about "assuming control" of your life, but what he offered was advice on how to abdicate control to God. Like a parent of children who never grow up, God is watchful, interventionist, always on call. No details of your life are too small for his attention; no decisions need be in your hands alone. No problems or conflicts need be confronted and resolved; you have only to ignore them. Peale's prescription for automatic behavior — regular recitations of affirmations and prayer — may deprive you of free will, but they absolve you of the anxiety that goes with it.

Forget your troubles and just be happy. We're used to hearing Peale's philosophy sung. He invokes a world of cheery artifice in which a smile is your best umbrella, and climbing every mountain, you never walk alone. "His optimism is too voluntary and defiant," William James complained of Walt Whitman,[8] and we might say the same of Peale, who borrowed liberally from late-nineteenth-century positive thinkers, proponents of "mind cure." Critiquing the mind-cure leaders of his day who preached "the all-saving power of healthy-minded attitudes" and warned against the "misery habit," James described the popularity of mind-cure principles that long preceded Peale:

> One hears of the 'Gospel of Relaxation,' of the 'Don't Worry Move ment,' of people who repeat to themselves, 'Youth, health, vigor!' when dressing in the morning, as their motto for the day. Com plaints of the weather are getting to be forbidden in many house holds; and more and more people are recognizing it to be bad form to speak of disagreeable sensations, or to make much of the ordinary inconveniences and ailments of life.[9]

James respected the utility of mind cure, recognizing that "the spread of the movement has been due to practical fruits," while he questioned what we might call its selfism: like the recovery movement, mind cure concerned itself only with individual, not social, health. But most of all James stressed the failure of positive thinkers to account for evil, which is, after all, "a genuine portion of reality."[10] Evil was merely a lie, a mispercep tion, according to believers in mind cure. Peale might put it down to bad attitudes.

Don't worry, be happy. If it is difficult to imagine many peo ple successfully obeying Peale's orders, it is frightening to con sider what might happen if they did. If conflict avoidance is a primary goal, democracy itself is a secondary one, not to men tion the justice that sometimes follows conflict resolution. The marketplace of ideas becomes a marketplace of maxims. Peale promises peace of mind, but it is the dull peace of the docile and the willfully oblivious.

Peale presented a vision of "consciousness trying *not* to be conscious," one of positive thinking's most incisive critics, Donald Meyer, has observed.[11] "Always express willingness to accept God's will," Peale stresses. "Ask for what you want but be willing to take what God gives you. It may be better than what you ask for." Thinking positively, you get to abdicate both judgment and will to God: "He guides your mind so that you do not want things that are not good for you or that are inharmonious with God's will."[12] Thinking positively, you may even abdicate desire.

It is clear that Peale was not addressing men and women with an interest in shaping their worlds or faith in their capacity to do so. The prototypical male who emerged from his book is the organization man of the 1950s, conformist, eager to learn the rules, anxious about his place in the hierarchy; the prototypical woman was his wife. What Peale promised men was ascension in the corporate world; he promised women that they could marry well: faith enhances beauty, he confirmed, as well as professional expertise ("God runs a beauty parlour").[13] Peale promoted the rigid delineation of sex roles that marked the 1950s: a woman who comes to him for advice on how to find a husband is gently chastised for her "domineering attitude." (She reproached Peale for arriving late for their appointment.)

> You have a very firm way of pressing your lips together.... I think you would be a very attractive person if you got those too-firm lines out of your face. You must have a little softness, a little tenderness, and those lines are too firm to be soft ... perhaps you could get that dress to hang a little better.... Perhaps it might help to get your hair fixed up a little. It's a little — floaty. Then you might also add a little sweet-smelling perfume.[14]

Like God, Peale is not above attending to details.

Indeed, the point of all his anecdotes is that faith has mundane, practical uses. Not only will it advance your career or marry you off, it will improve your golf swing and rid you of aches and pains. "From 50 to 75 percent of present-day people are ill because of the influence of improper mental states on their emotional and physical make-up," Peale reports, only a little nonsensically.[15]

" 'Do you know, I am beginning to realize that Christianity isn't theoretical after all,' " one of Peale's satisfied customers, "Bill," supposedly remarks. (All of Peale's conversants sound alike; that is, they sound like Peale.) Christianity is an applied science, Bill explains. "We have solved a problem according to well-defined spiritually scientific principles. I shudder to think of the terrible mistake we would have made had we not gone at this problem according to the formula contained in the teachings of Jesus."[16]

What was the problem they solved? Bill had been passed over for the presidency of his company. What was the scientific formula prescribed by Jesus? Peale's prayer for guidance and God's blessing and the plea that "Bill would be able to fit in with the new administration and give more effective service than before."[17] What was the outcome of this experiment in prayer? Bill was soon promoted to president after all.

Faith is the alchemy of Peale's system; faith is the "science" that spawns success and the spiritual well-being that supposedly goes with it. If nothing else, *The Power of Positive Thinking* offers a lesson in the technique of writing a best-selling self-help book: Promote the prevailing preoccupation of the time — the acquisition of either wealth or health — as the primary moral imperative. Package platitudes about positive thinking, prayer, or affirmation therapy as sure-fire, scientific techniques.

"Think and grow rich," Napoleon Hill wrote in 1936. Like *The Power of Positive Thinking*, *Think and Grow Rich* was a bestseller in its day and is still in print.[18] It is even available on tape cassettes, which I've seen advertised on late night TV. "Learn the secrets of the fabulously wealthy!" the announcers proclaim, while you ponder pictures of MasterCards and 800 telephone numbers. *Think and Grow Rich* is a lot like the Magic Weight Loss Belts, also advertised on late night (Not Available in Stores!) that Melt Off Pounds While You Sleep!

Napoleon Hill promised to reveal Andrew Carnegie's "magic formula" for getting rich. Hill claimed to have "analyzed hundreds of well known men" who had "accumulated their vast fortunes through the aid of the Carnegie secret," but he is a little coy about stating precisely what that secret is: "It has not been directly named, for it seems to work more successfully when it is merely uncovered and left in sight, where those who are ready, and searching for it, may pick it up."[19] Hill's book thus becomes a sort of treasure hunt, a test of the reader's persistence and worthiness to receive the truth.

Still, the secret is not so hard to grasp: "desire can be transmuted into gold. . . . riches begin with a state of mind." That message, intertwined with inspirational tales of positive thinking tycoons, is the gist of Hill's philosophy, which seems too good a parody of American materialism to be true. You must "truly *desire* money so keenly that your desire is an obsession," Hill declared, adding that America owed its freedom to men's obsession with wealth. "The benefactor of mankind is capital!" And, as the publisher's preface to *Think and Grow Rich* suggests, achievements in the world of capital bring "rich spiritual satisfaction."[20]

Hill's achievement was to present greed not just as a social and spiritual good but as the science of success. Greed turns itself into gold (as desire is "transmuted" into its "monetary equivalent"), Hill explained, through a scientific process involving the magnetic forces of thoughts, mixed with emotions, and through the mind's capacity for "attracting vibrations which harmonize with that which dominates the mind."[21] Weird physics:

Our brains become magnetized with the dominating thoughts which we hold in our minds, and, by means with which no man is familiar, these "magnets" attract to us the forces, the people, the circumstances of life which harmonize with the nature of our *dominating* thoughts.[22]

Faith is the magic ingredient of this mysterious process:

When faith is blended with thought, the subconscious mind instantly picks up the vibration, translates it into its spiritual equivalent, and transmits it to Infinite Intelligence, as in the case of prayer.[23]

How do you find faith? Like Norman Vincent Peale, Hill believed that faith was acquired automatically through the recitation of affirmations, repeated instructions to the "subconscious mind," or "autosuggestion."[24] In this world, you don't even need the will to believe, just the wish.

Hill is worth quoting at length, not because any of his statements makes sense but because none of them do; virtually impossible to satirize, he need only be quoted. We could dismiss him as a crank, if only he hadn't attracted so many readers; if only the "theories" he advanced hadn't already enjoyed considerable credibility in New Thought circles, one motto of which was "thoughts are things"; if only those same theories weren't still being recycled by New Age entrepreneurs like Werner Erhard, founder of est, who admits a debt to Napoleon Hill. Hill has reappeared most recently as the nominal coauthor of *Think and Grow Rich: A Black Choice*, a 1991 self-help book for the black community by Dennis Kimbra, a lecturer for the Napoleon Hill Foundation.

Not just a get-rich-quick scheme for late night television — in fact, hardly a scheme at all — Hill's book was a quasi-religious tract that reflected some widely accepted, if not quite mainstream, ideals. The goal of autosuggestion and control of your own subconscious mind was linking up with God, or, as Hill called Him, Infinite Intelligence. (God was mind, proponents of mind cure declared.) According to Hill, God was also a capitalist: Infinite Intelligence could be "induced to aid in transmuting desire into concrete, or material, form."[25] Carnegie's secret was getting God on his side.

Like most self-help authors, Hill makes rhetorical concessions to the ideal of self-control. He talks about mastering your fate by mastering your mind; but his notion of mastery seems mostly a matter of self-censorship: you have to stop yourself from thinking bad thoughts and becoming "failure conscious." Critical thinking is not just devalued by positive thinking philosophers; it is condemned as a barrier to God and success. Distinguishing between proper and improper thinking, Hill, Peale, and other mind-cure proselytizers were selling thought control, through "autosuggestion," not the free play of intelligence we might associate with self-actualization.* Preaching self-hypnosis, Hill and Peale assured readers that they could sleepwalk their way to wealth.

That is hardly what you'd call the Protestant ethic. Displacing the ideal of moral willfulness with the promise of wish fulfillment, positive thinking, or mind cure, has always been at odds with the liberal Protestant tradition that imagined success, achievement, and mastery of the environment as conscious acts of will. That tradition, not self-help movements like mind cure, reflected an ideal of self-invention. Liberal Protestantism's belief in the efficacy of individual will and individual action may have helped rationalize some of capitalism's abuses by exaggerating the capacity of the poor and disenfranchised to help themselves, but it also encouraged a belief in social reform. It is worth

*Abraham Maslow's work on self-actualization is discussed on pages 56–60.

noting that mind cure, which denigrated will and imagined we exist without it, was, as William James noted, not at all concerned with social ills or with the individual's relation to his or her community. Christian Science, the most widely known, still prospering offshoot of mind cure, was a church with no charitable endeavors, Mark Twain observed, in a scathing critique of it:

> I have hunted, hunted, and hunted, by correspondence and otherwise, and have not yet got upon the track of a farthing that the Trust has spent upon any worthy project. . . . No charities to support. No, nor even to contribute to. One searches in vain the Trust's advertisements and the utterances of its organs for any suggestion that it spends a penny on orphans, widows, discharged prisoners, hospitals, ragged schools, night missions, city missions, libraries, old people's homes, or any other object that appeals to a human being's purse through his heart.[26]

When will is devalued, so are action, independent thought, and social relations. We become atomized automatons, chanting affirmations, or the sayings of some expert that make very little sense. "In reality, the more closely error simulates truth and so-called matter resembles its essence, mortal mind, the more impotent error becomes as a belief," Mary Baker Eddy explained in *Science and Health*, her revelatory and supposedly infallible book.[27] As Twain observed, "She has a perfectly astonishing talent for putting words together in such a way as to make successful inquiry into their intention impossible."[28] But that hasn't stopped believers from quoting her. Conceiving of God as mind, and not will, Christian Science and mind cure generally conceived of men not as God's self-determining offspring with the potential to progress but as complete, self-enclosed "individualizations" of God.[29] This is not an entirely harmless religious belief: in the political realm, envisioning every man and woman as individualizations of the state is the essence of totalitarianism.

It is not that all positive thinkers are Stalinists or Nazis or that they present any imminent political threat. The inconsistencies of popular self-help movements, their tendency to draw from many sources, combining the mandate for surrender of will with appeals to individualism, make them less dangerous than movements that value ideological purity. But there is a strain of abnegation in the self-help tradition, represented most clearly in mind cure and positive thinking, that is essentially totalitarian.

■   ■   ■

One antidote for positive thinking and the lure of automatic behavior was the notion of self-actualization propounded by psychologist Abraham Maslow. While Peale spoke to men and women for whom identity was a matter of social status, who were liable to consider motivation, judgment, and creativity attributes of God, Maslow imagined independent, self-directed individuals who, given the freedom to choose, would always "choose wisely." He idealized "self-regulation, self-government," instead of submission:

> It is reasonable to assume in practically every human being, and certainly in almost every newborn baby, that there is an active will toward health, an impulse toward growth, or toward the actualization of human potentialities.[30]

> The human being is so constructed that he presses toward fuller and fuller being and this means pressing toward what most people would call good values, toward serenity, kindness, courage, honesty, love, unselfishness, and goodness.[31]

In this view, each of us has a unique inner nature that is either inherently good or, at least, morally neutral. (It is another irony of naming that Maslow presents a much more positive view of human nature than any positive thinker ever did.) Evil, social or individual, represents a frustration of basic inner needs. Neurosis is a "deficiency disease," a kind of psychic malnutrition.[32] (Peale's readers probably suffered from deficiency of desire.)

This sanguine belief in the capacity of people to grow in the right direction, once their basic needs for sustenance and security were met, was the essence of humanistic psychology, or the human potential movement, popularized by Maslow, Carl Rogers, and Gordon Allport at about the time that Peale was thinking his positive thoughts. Humanistic psychology offered a hopeful view of natural, individual potential, tempered by postwar awareness of the failures of social and political institutions. While Peale ignored the horrors of World War II, Maslow acknowledged them, briefly, but with some urgency: in the 1950s, he observed, Americans and Europeans were confronted with "the total collapse of all sources of values outside the individual."[33]

The goal of humanistic psychology was to uncover — not invent, Maslow stressed — a "natural value system. . . . There's no place else to turn but inward, to the self, as the locus of values."[34] Subjectivity was an obvious virtue, perhaps the cardinal virtue of this philosophy, that put every individual at the center of his or her own moral universe. The therapeutic relationship, therefore, was supposed to be nonauthoritarian and "client centered," Carl Rogers stressed. The role of the therapist was to facilitate growth without directing it.

This celebration of subjectivity was not relativism, as it is often assumed to be. Maslow did not suggest that all human behavior was healthy, only that all healthy behavior was self-directed. He idealized self-actualizers because he viewed them as moral "scouts" for the neurotic rest of us: "The healthiest people" are "more sensitive perceivers" who can "tell us less sensitive ones what it is that we value."[35] Only healthy people "yearn for what is good for them.... They spontaneously tend to do right, because that is what they *want* to do, what they *need* to do, what they enjoy, what they approve of doing."[36]

Maslow's concept of the self-actualized person is not entirely unlike the traditional religious concept of the person blessed with grace: when you accept God's love, you become infused with His will and His values. The truly faithful are capable only of doing what God wants; they want only the good. In some ways, Maslow simply relocated God, or some would say demoted Him, to a place within each individual. What distinguished self-actualizers was their embrace of the "godlike" in themselves.

Maslow was perhaps best known for his study of "peak experiences," moments of "ecstasy," generally associated with creative acts that are rungs on the ladder of self-actualization. He characterized these experiences in mystical terms: they entailed a loss of self-consciousness, a sense of existing "outside of time and space," a sense of "oneness," the perception of the universe as essentially benign or neutral, and what he described as a merger of values and facts: in peak experiences, there is no gap between what should be and what is. "Peakers," people who enjoyed more than the usual share of peak experiences, were subjective without being selfist: they tended to have callings or "vocations" that involved them with the world. The peak experience is a moment at which even "the average human being" is able to perceive other people and events objectively, independent of her own needs and desires. For peakers, "*perception can be relatively ego-transcending, self-forgetful, egoless.*"[37] Subjectivity was the route to self-actualization, but objectivity was its fruit.

Whatever charges may be leveled at Maslow — that he was an elitist who saw self-actualizers as the chosen few and favored "making life better" for the psychologically fit at the expense of the unfit[38] — he can't simply be called selfist or relativistic, nor can he be accused of simplifying the quest for identity; it would be fairer to say he mystified it. At least he didn't write how-to books. He couldn't have, not just because he was an academic writer, but because the ideal self-actualizer is an improviser, someone who doesn't need advice — road maps, role models, or assurances of success; she has the confident ability to "improvise in that situation which has never existed before."[39]

The how-to books of pop psychologists who followed Maslow appropriated the term *self-actualization* but mocked the concept, by devising guidelines and techniques for achieving it. Today, recovery experts borrowing Maslow's rhetoric about individual wholeness and autonomy promise self-actualization to anyone willing to follow directions for freeing the child within, as if, painting by numbers, we might each become Matisse. Adherence to externally devised, universally applicable techniques has about as much to do with self-actualization as reciting a poem has to do with writing one.

Maslow's theories were more aptly adopted by political activists of the 1960s, for whom Maslow had little patience or respect. The Port Huron Statement, the seminal declaration of belief for the student movement, lauded "self-cultivation, self-direction, self-understanding, and creativity," calling for an iconoclastic "quality of mind . . . which openly faces problems which are troubling and unresolved; one with an intuitive awareness of possibilities, an active sense of curiosity, and ability and willingness to learn."[40] As the sober passion of this statement drew on Maslow's hint that self-actualizers might save the world, Abbie Hoffman's playful anarchism drew on the respect for individual intimations of delight that his work demanded. To recover the self, Maslow wrote, "one must recover the ability to perceive one's own delights."[41] Hoffman delighted in revolution, revolution for the fun of it, fun being "an experience so intense that you are actualizing your full potential. . . . I like to experience pleasure. Just doing what pops into my mind. I trust my impulse," he declared.[42] His pitch for the revolution went like this:

> Look, you want to have more fun, you want to get laid more, you want to turn on with your friends, you want an outlet for your creativity, then get out of school, quit your job. Come on out and help build and defend the society you want. Stop trying to organize everybody but yourself. Begin to live your vision.[43]

Hoffman acknowledged Maslow's clear influence, to the latter's apparent chagrin.[44]

But if Abraham Maslow disliked the way in which his ideas were used by radicals of the 1960s, it is hard to agree that he was misunderstood. In his work, he located conscience and morality in individuals, not in their political institutions; he linked ethical behavior with self-awareness (therapy itself was a "search for values"); he made the development of individual potential a moral imperative, while recognizing that "good human beings will generally need a good society in which to grow."[45] Abbie Hoffman had the courage of Maslow's convictions.

Putting faith in the individual, however idealized, humanistic psychology implicitly valued dissent over conformity and presented willful individual action not just as a possibility but as a virtue, providing a theory of individual development that encouraged the formation of political community — the "democracy of individual participation" envisioned by the Port Huron Statement. The humanistic psychologists shaped the primary postwar philosophy of identity formation that can fairly be classed as self-help and reflected democratic ideals, which eventually limited its commercial appeal. Valuing iconoclasm and a spirit of improvisation, the theory of self-actualization could never compete in the marketplace of techniques. Nor could it survive intact the notion that personal development required little unselfish social interaction, which we've come to know as the selfism of the past twenty years. In the 1970s, self-actualization easily devolved into a pseudoscience of self-aggrandizement.

In *How to Get Whatever You Want Out of Life*, written in 1978, Dr. Joyce Brothers combined positive thinking with the rhetoric of self-actualization in a best-selling primer on making dreams come true.[46] Only you, the "inner you," can "truly know" what you want out of life, Brothers concedes, and only she, it seems can teach you how to get it. "Love, power, riches, success, a good marriage, exciting sex, fulfillment . . . can be yours, if you want them," if you buy her book. "A how-to book can make all the difference," Brothers shamelessly declares.[47]

Her how-to book offers the usual array of platitudes, pep talks, and case studies about wishing and hoping and thinking your way to success and self-actualization, which by now means "a more rewarding lifestyle." She dresses this up in "scientific techniques," like the Quick List Technique: Write down three wishes, just "as fast as you can," without reflection, she urges, just like a fairy godmother. But she is a scientist, and the Quick List Technique is a "powerful psychological tool." As proof of its potency, Brothers tells the story of "Norman," who, after writing a quick wish list, transforms himself from a middle-class salesman into a wealthy entrepreneur, proud owner of "a metallic silver sports car with red leather upholstery."[48] Your wish list should, apparently, be quite specific.

Brothers's advice is quite specific too. In her collection of special, psychological learning techniques, she devises a study schedule for you: "Eat a light supper and start working at six. . . . Stop working at 8:30 for a half an hour. . . . During this half hour have a cup of decaffeinated coffee or weak tea or an apple. . . . And no alcohol." Another learning secret is studying in a cool, quiet room: "Mental activity thrives on a chilly atmosphere, so keep the room on the cold side — 60 to 65° is most conducive to learning." Brothers also shares her own study secret: "I have written most of this book on airplanes," she confides,[49] and I believe her.

It is easy to understand the appeal of these assurances that concentration and creativity are merely functions of turning the thermostat down. It is harder to imagine readers pondering banalities because they are presented as techniques — but some do. That is the secret of the doctor's success. "You will learn more and faster . . . if you settle down in the same room at the same desk at the same time every time you study," she declares. "This helps you condition yourself to study in very much the same way that Pavlov taught his dog to salivate when it heard a bell."[50] Brothers talks about self-actualization, but, like Norman Vincent Peale, she is really a Pavlovian. She presents her own psychological expertise as "tools" for manipulating yourself and others.

"The ability to manipulate effectively is the key to power," she reports in chapters on how to succeed.[51] Brothers notes in her introductory chapters that money can buy happiness only "up to a point," but that's the point she'll help you reach; the acquisition of money and power turn out to be her primary subjects.

Like an employment counselor, she offers tips on job interviews: don't smoke, don't be late, make sure you know the name of the person interviewing you. A woman of the world, she encourages you to exploit your connections: "It's whom you know that counts," she confirms. She is pragmatic and essentially amoral: "It is relatively easy to manipulate people through guilt," she observes; and although the exercise is "quite distasteful," she must admit that it is an important psychological tool.[52]

Brothers devotes a chapter to "How to Make People Do What You Want." She'll help you become a "power person" who knows how to use the "most effective psychological tools" for manipulating people: "flattery, rewards, guilt, and fear — in that order." Flattery is one of her favorites: "Everyone has an inferiority complex," so everyone is susceptible to a practiced flatterer who knows how to exploit insecurities. "Zero in on those areas of real concern to the person being flattered . . . bolster his ego in areas where he may feel unsure," Brothers advises. Practice her "sensitive listening techniques."[53]

Write you own "manipulative handbook," she concludes. It will help you gain power and friends.[54]

Like most successful self-help experts, Brothers synthesizes the sayings of her predecessors. "There is power in thinking," she exclaims;[55] Peale and Dale Carnegie seem her strongest influences. And she plays to the tune of the times. In the late 1970s it was fulfillment through professional success, for women as well as men. A social conscience seemed quaint and awfully naive, and dissent was no longer in fashion. If humanistic psychology dominated the 1960s, positive thinking reigned again in the late 1970s, most notably in the virulent form of est. Est's phenomenal success reflected an emerging preoccupation with private fulfillment at the expense of public welfare.

Werner Erhard, aka Jack Rosenberg, founded est after an alleged epiphany on a California freeway: "I realized that I knew nothing. . . . In the next instant — after I realized that I knew nothing — I realized that I knew everything. . . . It was so stupidly, blindingly simple that I could not believe it. I saw that there were no hidden meanings, that everything was just the way it is, and that I was already all right. All that knowledge that I had amassed just obscured the simplicity, the truth, the suchness, the thusness of it all." He felt obliged to "share" this revelation with others and built an empire.[56]

As his fluency in psychobabble indicates, before becoming a leader in the personal development field Erhard was one of its most voracious consumers. He read Napoleon Hill and acknowledged him as a major influence: "I know that some people make fun of persons like Napoleon Hill," Erhard told a biographer. "But if you really look at what [he] had to say you find integrity and humanity." Then, having immigrated to California in the 1960s, Erhard "encountered" the human potential movement, learned to employ its rhetoric, and became a peaker: "The peak experience that I had in 1963 was a peak experience of what I call Self. . . . I truly experienced *the* Self — not *my* Self: the word 'my' belongs in the world of *concept* about Self not *experience* of Self." He moved on and through Zen Buddhism and Scientology, another major influence: "not until I encountered Scientology did I see clearly that Mind is at the root of all the trouble; and that the trouble lies in its positionality." Finally he took a Dale Carnegie course on how to win friends and influence people. Erhard was, after all, a salesman by profession.[57]

With his talent for salesmanship and forays into practically every important, modern personal development movement, Erhard was a quintessentially American phenomenon; he was invented by the self-help culture he came to lead. Shallow and glib, he blended the rhetorics of several different movements into a babble all his own and convinced people that he was saying something different, which couldn't have been much harder than convincing them that he was saying something.

Like Napoleon Hill, Erhard essentially claimed to have discovered a way to "think and grow rich." Est promised grandly to "transform your ability to experience life," as Barbara Grizzuti Harrison reported in a witty and unsettling 1976 exposé.[58] This meant shifting "from a state in which the content in your life is organized around the attempt to get satisfied or to survive . . .

to an experience of *being* satisfied, right now, and organizing the content of your life as an expression, manifestation, and sharing of the experience of being satisfied, of being whole and complete, now."[59] Get it? You don't really have to. Beneath the senseless, lofty rhetoric, Erhard's message was the same one Hill was selling back in 1936: Desire can be turned into gold. Thoughts are things. Expectations are always self-fulfilling.

Erhard's epiphany, I suspect, was that the mass marketing of these secrets would be greatly enhanced by making them expensive and painful to obtain. Est training sessions had the mystique of boot camp or fraternity hazings. Trainees paid hundreds of dollars for the privilege of being imprisoned together in large rooms and subject to psychic drills and verbal harangues: "You are all assholes," est trainers would proclaim.[60] The widely publicized fact that trainees were denied free access to bathrooms only seemed to heighten est's appeal. Training was an ordeal that, once survived, stamped you as one of the elite.

There is no way to know what every est graduate gleaned from this training. People came to est, as they come to any self-help program, with their own idiosyncratic temperaments, desires, and ideas. Some claim convincingly that they found in est a sense of "personal empowerment" that inspired social activism. But I suspect that they entered est with a social conscience already formed and managed to leave with it still intact. The popular message of est, the one that reverberated throughout the culture, was a clear denigration of compassion.

We are in complete control of our lives and are completely responsible for our successes and failures, est proselytizers proclaimed. There is no such thing as luck (positive thinkers don't generally believe in luck), which means that there are no hapless victims, only assholes who invite their own abuse. Est offered noblesse without the oblige; wealth brought with it no responsibilities if people were poor voluntarily (because they liked sleeping on grates). It was the perfect philosophy for a decade in which success began replacing social justice as the predominant cultural ideal. No one deserves your help and no one could effectively make use of it, est declared. Character is fate absolutely.

Character takes shape in a vacuum. If the recovery movement is obsessed with the effect of family life on character, est ignored it, along with all other circumstances beyond our control. In Erhard's universe, we are each our own creation. If recovery makes victims of us all, est gave us permission to be predators.

Although recovery experts use positive thinking techniques — affirmations and visualizations — and parrot sayings about mind power, they don't borrow much positive thinking ideology. Tracing the historical roots of a self-help movement is often difficult because experts borrow so illogically from a range of popular movements that preceded them. But ideologically, the recovery movement owes more to popular Protestant notions of salvation by grace and nineteenth-century revivalism, while est is deeply rooted in mind cure. Neither offers a balanced, nuanced view of our responsibility for ourselves and our environments; neither offers the possibility of willful, moral action. But while recovery may be irritating and adolescent, est was cruel.

Erhard's philosophy clearly demonstrated the antisocial strain of the positive thinking/mind-cure tradition, which Mark Twain saw reflected in the Christian Science neglect of charity. If each of us creates our own reality, then each of us is entirely self-sufficient, self-enclosed, like the individuations of God that mind cure imagined us to be. Erhard reaffirmed, with a vengeance, the message of Norman Vincent Peale: there are no social ills, no external forces affecting our fates; there is only negative thinking, the enemy within. Regrets are unnecessary because you need only desire success to achieve it. Compassion is a waste of psychic energy.

Today, est is available in a kinder, gentler package called The Forum. Participants in Forum seminars have free access to bathrooms and are spared some of the verbal abuse once heaped on est trainees. But the message to be extracted from The Forum's New Age rhetoric about such phenomena as experiential receptors of beingness is the same: You are whole. You are complete. You are the writer, director, and star of a one-person play.

If bad things happen only to people guilty of thinking bad thoughts, then evil is, as mind-cure leaders claimed, a mistake, a misapprehension; evil is a lie. (Or, as Mary Baker Eddy put it: "Evil is the awful deception and unreality of existence."[61]) There are, then, no tragedies, no awful accidents of fate; there are no conflicts of wills, only errors of perception, and no injustice. Mind cure, positive thinking, and est don't offer a reading of the Book of Job so much as a rejection of it.

The failure to confront or even admit the existence of evil makes mind cure, or positive thinking, "inadequate as a philosophy," as William James stressed. But James was being kind. Denying the existence of evil, it is a Faustian philosophy that grants placidity of mind in exchange for empathy and the will to alleviate suffering.

James was tolerant of mind cure and respectful of its practical successes, but he was not drawn to it. Mind cure was unheroic, he concluded; it required too little of us and deprived us of "the strenuous life" of mortal conflict in service to ideals: "There is an element of real wrongness in this world, which is neither to be ignored nor evaded, but which must be squarely met and overcome by an appeal to the soul's heroic resources, and neutralized and cleansed away by suffering."[62]

FOUR

In Step:
Support Groups

At a Sex and Love Addicts Anonymous (SLAA) meeting, a bearded, middle-aged man confesses that he masturbated last week. "But it's okay. I'm okay with it," he assures us. He is beginning to understand that when he masturbates he is "acting out" his anger. Now, in recovery, he is in the process of "getting in touch" with his anger, and it is healing his addiction to sex.

Everyone in this small group of fifteen or sixteen people, seated in a circle, nods. Then Pamela, a young woman who is "powerless over relationships," tells of her struggles not to call her ex-boyfriend, with whom she just broke up last month. It is hard for her to be alone. She misses "not the sex but the touching" and wonders if her desire to be held is "part of my disease." The nodding continues. Recovering sex addict Joanne talks about using sex to gain control. Amy talks about being out of control in relationships. Carl tells us about his bad day at work and his feelings of worthlessness, which underlie his promiscuity. "I definitely use sex to make myself feel wanted and important," he confides with less originality than conviction. Now he is trying to stop and is practicing his affirmations: "I keep reminding myself that I'm not a bad person. I'm an addict, a sick, suffering person," he says, seeking self-esteem.

Meanwhile, a few blocks away, in another church basement, recovering alcoholics are telling harrowing stories of blackouts and binges. A few blocks in another direction, recovering over-eaters are talking about loving their bodies. Several hours after these lunchtime meetings, within the same half-mile radius, Adult Children of Alcoholics (ACOA), Narcotics Anonymous (NA), and Codependents Anonymous (CODA) will hold their meetings. In my town and probably in yours, there are lunch-time, evening, and sometimes morning meetings, five to seven days a week, for twelve-step groups addressing every conceivable form of addiction, every bad habit, every complaint.

The stories you hear range quickly from the trivial to the tragic. As soon as one woman finishes testifying to the ravages of PMS, another recalls being raped by her stepfather. Disparate, disconnected stories come in quick succession; sometimes attending groups is like watching MTV. But while the testimony changes, the mood of the group — somber — is fairly constant. Everyone's story is greeted with equal seriousness and shows of concern. (Remember, all suffering is relative.)

The format of the groups is also constant. (They're like 7-eleven stores; you can walk into a twelve-step group anywhere in the country, I suspect, and feel at home.) Members take turns leading the meetings; usually they begin by reading the Alco-holics Anonymous Serenity Prayer: "God grant me the serenity to accept the things I cannot change, courage to change the things I can, and wisdom to know the difference." Then the leader reads a mission statement, also taken from AA, affirm-ing that the group is "a fellowship of men and women who share their experience, strength and hope with each other that they may solve their common problem and help others to recover." The statement includes a disavowal of any religious or political affiliation or any membership requirement other than the desire to recover.

Virtually all recovery groups use the same twelve steps, which are essentially a series of maxims and mandates, originated by AA. Step one is a statement of need: "We admitted we were powerless over _____" (fill in alcohol, drugs, food, sex, shopping, gambling, or religion, or any particular feeling, such as sadness or rage). Step twelve is a statement of success and commitment to evangelicism: "Having had a spiritual awakening as a result of these steps, we tried to carry this message to other _____ [alcoholics, drug abusers, rageoholics, shoppers, etc.] and to practice these principles in all of our affairs." Steps in between include making "a searching and fearless moral inventory," "humbly" asking God to "remove our shortcomings," and making "moral amends" to "all persons we have harmed." Accompanying these twelve steps are twelve traditions, also suitable for use in recovering from any addiction. Tradition one is a statement of allegiance to the group: "Our common welfare should come first; personal recovery depends upon unity." Tradition two vows allegiance to a generic, "loving God as He may express Himself in our group conscience." Other traditions include respect for anonymity, and prohibition of commercial ventures and outside contributions to the group. "Our public relations policy is based on attraction rather than promotion," according to tradition eleven.

Many thoughtful people study these steps and are helped by them. Many find in them not a mandate to submit but a call for personal accountability. I realize, of course, that my reading of the twelve steps is not the only one and that an outsider's analysis of them and other recovery credos may not matter much to someone struggling with an addiction to alcohol or drugs who finds the program helpful.

Although I'm instinctively skeptical of recovery and other personal development movements, I'm not a critic of recovery's forerunner — AA — any more than a supporter of it. I am quite critical of our expanded definitions of addiction and the many derivative twelve-step groups for people suffering not from chemical addictions but from what might be considered bad habits or neuroses — overeating and "loving too much." But I've known people who destroyed themselves with alcohol or drugs and others who have recovered through AA. I've read convincing personal accounts of recovery from alcoholism that I have not the intention, desire, or capacity to refute. I've attended AA meetings on Christmas Day and been impressed by the fellowship they offered people. Observing AA and NA groups as a nonparticipant, I have only a limited view of the recovery process. I know I'm not privy to the friendships that form in AA: one recovering alcoholic tells me that the meetings are not nearly as important to him as the socializing that follows them.

So I don't claim that my remarks about twelve-step groups are dispositive; they are simply my remarks, reflecting my reaction to these groups. I'm not offering arguments about treatments of chemical addictions. I do want to provide a more critical, political perspective on the twelve-step phenomenon than is popularly considered.

The twelve steps that so many people find helpful are stultifying to me. Imagine listening to the same serenity prayer, the same steps and traditions, at every meeting you attend. After reading the serenity prayer and mission statement, the leader usually passes around a statement of the twelve traditions that people take turns reading. For me, this is the hardest part to sit through; people read dead words in monotones. A few recovering alcoholics I know say they never listen to the opening mantras either, but I guess that many others are comforted by the ritual readings, as they are comforted by familiar prayers in church.

You can only guess what most people in recovery feel about these and other rituals. We have anecdotal testimony about the redemptive force of the twelve steps but no hard evidence of their general effect. It is probably impossible to know much about the millions of disparate, anonymous individuals who move in and out of support groups unpredictably, with varying degrees of success. Support groups are quite permeable, perhaps the most permeable of all our private associations, lacking membership requirements or even membership lists. They are the most laissez-faire of private associations, setting forth general standards of behavior that tend to be obeyed rather than actively enforced. You may be excommunicated from your church or blackballed by a country club, but it is virtually impossible to be denied entry to a group or excluded from the community of twelve steppers. Even if you outrage the people who regularly attend one meeting, you can always move on to another.

So the abundance of anecdotal reports on twelve-step groups is matched by a dearth of empirical evidence about their memberships. I've never even found a reliable demographic study of twelve-step groups; my evidence also is mainly anecdotal.

The majority of groups I've attended have been mostly white and middle-class, as is the neighborhood in which I live. Except for those that meet in hospitals serving diverse populations, support groups seem to reflect the demographics of their neighborhoods. (Attending AA groups in the wealthy part of town has long been heralded as a way to snag a wealthy spouse.) AA groups used to be all male, but now they welcome women, who made up about half of the AA groups I observed. Codependents Anonymous and Overeaters Anonymous were predominantly female. AA and Narcotics Anonymous groups were the most diverse in terms of race, gender, and, I think, class: people who appeared working-class mingled with people who seemed relatively rich. Meetings of Codependents Anonymous, Sex and Love Addicts Anonymous, Overeaters Anonymous, and Adult Children of Alcoholics were the most homogeneous. In general, addiction may be a great equalizer, but some people apparently feel safer with what they consider to be their own kind. Groups sometimes serve very discrete populations, such as nonsmoking lesbian mothers of sons.

What may be harder to find are recovery groups that don't refer you to God or your higher power, although a few for recovering alcoholics have recently emerged. The drive for secular recovery, from alcoholism at least, may even be considered a movement: Newsweek has made it the subject of a "lifestyle" story. (It's fueled partly by the tendency of judges to sentence drunken drivers to recovery programs; some consider a sentence to AA a violation of religious freedom.) Rational Recovery, a leading secular alcohol recovery group affiliated with the American Humanist Association, has spread to 150 cities, according to Newsweek.[1]

Still, Rational Recovery boasts only two thousand members at any given time, compared with the one million plus membership of AA.[2] Women for Sobriety, another secular recovery group, claims some five thousand members,[3] but in my town, where there are AA meetings virtually every day of the week, the local Women for Sobriety chapter has folded. There is a market for secular recovery, but it may have limited resilience in a country in which atheism is considered unpatriotic. Just as the business of America is business, religion is America's religion.[4]

I've never attended a support group that didn't call on a higher power; how seriously people in recovery take Him I cannot say. Some recovering alcoholics say they "tune out" all references to God, along with some testimony and whatever steps or traditions they don't "relate to." I suspect that the people who benefit most from recovery are the savviest, most selective consumers of it — the ones who don't share in everything that goes on in the group and who ignore much of what the experts say.

I suspect, I guess, I imagine. Suspicions, guesses, and impressions constitute much of what we know about support groups. Because the support group movement is so difficult to document, like most people writing about it, I can only comment on what I've seen.

■   ■   ■

The Narcotics Anonymous meeting at a local hospital begins with the reading of the serenity prayer, mission statement, and the twelve traditions. People read haltingly, flatly, as people unaccustomed to reading aloud often do. Finally the twelfth tradition has been read, and the leader moves on to welcome "newcomers to the group." Several newcomers stand up and introduce themselves, including a contingent from Baltimore: "I'm George, and I'm a drug addict from Baltimore," one man says, and everyone applauds. "I'm Bob, and I'm a drug addict from Baltimore," the man sitting next to him says, to more applause. Two more men from Baltimore and a couple from Worcester are welcomed. I have had a bad week — ended both a job and a relationship — and for an instant, just an instant that takes me by surprise, I have an impulse to stand up and say, "I'm Wendy, and I'm a drug addict from New York."

Then the testimony begins, and the group's relationship to language changes. Instead of reciting someone else's words, people are struggling to find their own. Many testifiers are inelegant and their vocabularies are limited: every other sentence is punctuated by a "fuck." But speaking their own words, detailing their own anguished bouts with addiction, they are eloquent. One man who says he has been straight for six months speaks movingly of being watched over physically by members of his group, intent on not letting him score. I imagine him hanging over a cliff, with the group holding onto his ankles. He gives me a new, less skeptical appreciation of support.

No one talks about God much at this meeting. His name comes up only during the prayer and recitation of traditions. No one testifies to his or her relationship with God or thanks Him for His help, which distinguishes this from many other meetings I've attended.

There is a good more God talk in AA. "My higher power did for me what I could not do for myself," I hear one man say, describing God's miraculous intervention in his life. "On my own, I was unable to stop drinking. And when I first came [to AA], I didn't believe in God, and when I asked Him for help I was just going through the motions." Then he underwent a conversion. "I sank to my knees and admitted I was powerless and cried, 'God, if you're there, please help me,' and He did."

If you are not religious, testimony like this may be grating, like the screech of chalk on a blackboard. If you are not religious but in need of AA, this may be what you learn to "tune out" — the frequent exhortations about surrendering to a higher power, discussions of the "spiritual bankruptcy" that precedes conversion to AA, and the grateful encomiums to His benefi-cence. Sitting through religious testimonials, I'm grateful that I'm not an alcoholic and don't have to sit through religious testimonials. But a couple of agnostics I know who credit their recovery to AA dismiss its religiosity as a minor irritation. Unlike organized religions, they suggest, recovery is indeed a cafeteria.

Freedom not to pay attention, along with the freedom to drop in and out of meetings as you choose, are the saving graces of AA and other twelve-step groups. Flexibility and lack of organizational controls distinguish recovery from cults. Many people, I imagine, actively question recovery's teachings, bending them to suit their needs, but it is impossible to know how many. Watching participants in a recovery conference nodding at the experts, taking notes on their one-liners, never asking questions or disputing their assertions, I see little evidence of people actively processing and critiquing recovery's message. Attending support groups, I hear people echoing the experts, talking about getting in touch with their anger or letting go of it; they seem to practice talk show therapy on themselves.

In twelve-step groups, I've encountered what appears to be a nervous, needy, vulnerable population, eager to believe. I don't expect an undereducated twenty-year-old with a history of drug and alcohol abuse and intermittent homelessness to analyze recovery's ideology, particularly if she finds that it helps. I understand her gratitude for the group and its value to her: "It's great to talk and not worry about someone thinking you're stupid," one young woman says poignantly, recounting her adolescent years of drinking, blacking out, and waking up in strange apartments, with only a few odd still-lifes to indicate where she might have been. Hearing people testify to the ravages of drug and alcohol abuse, I lose some of my skepticism about the groups that seem to help them. At the same time I wonder how limited their own capacity for skepticism might be.

At an Adult Children of Alcoholics meeting, people testify to their inability to "handle" mundane complications and annoyances of daily life — checking accounts that won't balance, files at work that won't be found, friends who borrow books and don't return them. They discuss the dynamics of "dealing" with bank managers, auto mechanics, and acquaintances the way I imagine foreign policy advisers discuss an upcoming summit. Should you ask your neighbor to pick up your mail when you go on vacation? How should you pose the question and initiate the "process" of negotiation? Should you be relying on your neighbor? Can you trust him with your mailbox key and will he expect a favor in return? You'd like to ask a friend who lives across town to check your mail instead, but you're afraid of appearing too needy.

How do these people get through the day, I wonder, listening to them agonize about the nuances of every trivial human encounter, thanking my higher power I'm not a therapist.

I realize that many people in recovery are genuinely unhappy and deeply confused about human relations, having been damaged, or at least dented, early on in childhood. Some people are as debilitated by inconveniences as others are by crises. Still, my capacity for sympathy is sometimes limited. The problems you hear discussed in ACOA and CODA meetings don't seem nearly as formidable as the problems of the poor and uninsured chronically ill. Listening to thirty-five-year-olds complain that they have never been understood by their parents, I find myself thinking about the Kurds.

Am I being unfair or unrealistic? As a legal aid lawyer, I represented people facing serious felony charges and people with summonses for not paying their subway fares. It may only be the equivalent of a traffic ticket, I'd remind myself when a farebeat asked anxiously about his case, but it is his traffic ticket. "They may only be imperfect parents," an ACOA might say, "but they are my imperfect parents."

Unfortunately, that's precisely what ACOAs and other people in recovery tend not to say (at least not one of them has ever said it to me). They're more likely to complain that their parents are not merely imperfect but abusive. They're more likely to insist that their problems are not simply their problems but our problems too, the symptoms of a social disease. Virtually all American families are dysfunctional, we live in a dysfunctional society, recovery experts proclaim, effectively assuring people that virtually all their personal problems are automatically worthy of public attention.

Outside their support groups, people are testifying too, in the most inappropriate places. At cocktail parties and in casual encounters with acquaintances, they tell their unsolicited life stories, proffering intimacies like calling cards. Sometimes in a public forum — a book reading or a discussion of safe streets — someone in recovery seizes an opportunity to share her pain. Feelings and personal experiences are competing with ideas in academia as well. At a lecture on psychoanalytic theory, people stand up during the question and answer period and testify to their histories of abuse. "My mother sodomized me," one man declares repeatedly, regaling us with some graphic detail. Five or ten more people — I lose count — stand up and identify themselves as victims of abuse, while the audience murmurs and nods respectfully. (At least no one applauds.) I wonder what testifiers mean by abuse. Were they sodomized by their mothers too or merely "shamed," deprived of self-esteem? I doubt they ask themselves if this audience of strangers really cares about their problems. They either presume our support or demand it. In recovery the self becomes a social issue.

The tendency of people in recovery to imbue their particular stories with general public importance, imagining them to be of public interest, was also a hallmark of early feminist support groups. But from the beginning, consciousness raising was accompanied by political action. The recovery movement lacks even a political agenda, much less concern about the rights and responsibilities of citizenship. In recovery it is not just that the personal is political; the political is merely personal.

The self-aggrandizement that follows from this conflation of personal and political problems helps distinguish recovery from traditional psychotherapy and the innumerable support groups that aren't modeled on AA. The language of recovery is pervasive, but not all support groups are twelve-step groups. Coexisting with recovery groups are groups for people in crisis — people confronting cancer or a death in the family or divorce. Formed in response to events and traumas in people's lives, not the chronic condition of codependency, these groups are not generally in the business of promoting theories of selfhood, much less visions of sin and redemption. In general, they're not evangelical.

Not that support groups outside the recovery movement aren't widespread. *Newsweek* estimates that fifteen million Americans attend support groups, twelve-step or not.[5] The basis of this estimate is unclear: how do you count an anonymous and ever-changing population? But I'm willing to believe that support groups outside recovery do involve millions of people. You can probably find a no-step group for every conceivable segment of the population, from parents opposed to circumcision to people who have been visited by aliens. (Twelve-step groups don't have a copyright on silliness.) But lacking a cohesive ideology, these groups do not constitute an identifiable personal development movement. Some are therapeutic, of course, but given the range of interests, causes, and problems they address, groups outside recovery are best viewed simply as part of the larger, pluralistic tradition of private associations.

It is, therefore, even more difficult to generalize about support groups that don't follow AA's twelve steps. I've focused on twelve-step groups primarily because they do contribute to a national movement with an insidious jargon and ideology and partly because twelve-step groups are anonymous and usually open to the public.

But attending several twelve-step meetings a week, listening to people talk about their parents and their PMS, I needed to listen to people grappling with more awesome problems. Of course, some of the problems you hear aired in twelve-step groups are awesome enough, like the problems of alcoholics, drug addicts, and incest victims; it's just that I find the rhetoric of recovery unrevealing and the ideology disturbing. So, as an antidote to recovery, I visited groups of Cambodian women refugees — women who were persecuted by the Khmer Rouge regime, women who survived torture, starvation, multiple rapes, and internment in concentration camps and witnessed the slaughter of their families, women who endured what I can't imagine. The Khmer Rouge is reported to have killed about one million people betwen 1975 and 1979, the years they remained in power.

These women are the Holocaust survivors to whom some recovering codependents, like John Bradshaw, compare themselves. Many people in recovery tell "trauma stories" and have seized upon the syndrome afflicting these refugees — posttraumatic stress disorder — and claimed it as their own. (Virtually all codependents are said by the experts to be victims of PTSD.) If some recovering codependents resent my comparing them to Cambodian refugees whose sufferings they cannot match, I'm making the comparison their movement has invited.

I'm not suggesting that we should ignore all lesser degrees of suffering and care only about greater ones or that only torture victims and targets of genocide have reason to be unhappy and the right to be heard, but they do have more reason and perhaps we should afford them greater rights. Mostly, I offer this portrait of Cambodian women refugees as a reality check, a reminder of the difference between holocausts that happen only metaphorically and holocausts that happen in fact.

Unlike many ACOAs and other people in recovery, these Cambodian survivors don't glibly proffer their stories to strangers. Their relative silence reflects, in part, a difference between Asian and American cultures: discussing emotional problems with strangers or even clinicians is not part of the Indochinese tradition. Their reticence also reflects, I suspect, the severity of the traumas they have suffered. How do you testify casually, facilely, to torture and genocide?

So, although I have sat in on several group sessions, I have only heard the individual trauma stories of these women secondhand, from their doctors and social workers. I find the details hard to remember, probably because they are so horrific and hard to absorb. For some reason, I only recall the story of a woman who watched soldiers split her husband's head open with an axe and was spared, unaccountably, after being forced to dig her own grave. The literature on Indochinese refugees includes stories like this: A woman sees her parents disemboweled; she is beaten, tossed on the bodies of her relatives, and left to die. A ten-year-old girl is interned in a work camp until she is fifteen; she is regularly beaten, tortured (once she was hung by her ankles from a tree for three days), kept in solitary confinement for months, and raped repeatedly. A man who was interned and tortured is the sole survivor of his family of forty-seven people.[6]

Survivors of the Khmer Rouge are, in general, multiple trauma victims. "Khmer psychiatric patients in the United States have experienced an average of 16 major trauma events," according to a 1989 U.N. report: "The traumatic experiences of these patients fall into four general categories: 1) deprivation; 2) physical injury and torture; 3) incarceration, brainwashing, re-education camps; and 4) witnessing killings or torture."[7]

The traumas did not end with the fall of the Khmer Rouge in 1979. Over 300,000 Cambodians still live as displaced persons in camps along the Thailand border. Conditions in the camps are supposed to be "humane enough to protect the physical well-being of the Khmer but harsh enough to discourage other Cambodians from seeking refuge in Thailand." In fact, inmates in the camps are beset by chronic malnutrition, crime, poverty, domestic violence, and shellings from ongoing border conflicts. Confinement in a camp is described as "re-victimization and re-traumatization" by U.N. observers.[8]

For those lucky enough to experience it, emigration to the United States is traumatic too. None of the Cambodian women I encountered spoke more than a few words of English; meetings are bilingual, and a bilingual Indochinese health worker mediates the relationship between the groups and American clinicians. All of the women are poor and live in communities with high homicide, robbery, and arson rates. For some, simply traveling to the clinic once or twice a week is difficult: the subways are frightening and confusing, and many women who have suffered multiple rapes are afraid of taking cabs for fear of being alone with the drivers. One meeting I attended occurred only a few days after a Cambodian woman in their neighborhood was robbed and murdered in her apartment and during a spate of fires that left many families homeless. The women discuss their fears and practice dialing 911, saying "emergency" and reciting their American addresses. They are scared and a little somber until a raucous older woman exhorts them to toughen up, acting out how she intends to greet anyone who tries breaking into her house; shrieking fearlessly, she makes everybody laugh.

There is more laughter and lightness in these meetings of vulnerable, impoverished survivors of genocide than in any twelve-step group I've attended, where people pursue recovery with deadening earnestness. Twelve-step groups depress me — so many people talking about such relatively trivial problems with such seriousness, in the same nonsensical jargon. The Cambodian women's groups impress and enhearten me — such resilience these women show.

These are not classic self-help groups; they are organized and directed by health care professionals. But they are directed democratically and seem more like support groups than traditional group therapy. Groups are unstructured and informal. One group meets in a rundown community center; twenty or twenty-five of us crowd into a small room and share the floor. They are social events; another group concludes its meetings with an enormous, communal, potluck lunch. Socializing and socialization — education in American customs and rules — takes perhaps as much time as what might formally be considered therapy — people talking about how they feel. In some ways, the clinic that organized these groups reminds me of turn-of-the-century settlement houses that served an earlier, less traumatized population of immigrants.

There are many obvious differences between professionally led groups for Cambodian refugees and leaderless recovery groups. But the structural differences (or similarities) between refugee and recovery groups are not relevant to my concern, which is this: the hierarchy of suffering that the recovery movement denies and the cult of victimization it encourages.

Unlike many twelve steppers I've heard, the Cambodian women don't seem to revel in their victimhood. Their meetings aren't collections of complaints and testimonies about their pain. Sometimes they are sad and serious; sometimes the sadness is an interruption in a long moment of frivolity. At one session the women practice putting makeup on each other. At another, they experiment with sample gifts of body lotion, discussing approaches to skin care like leisured ladies at a spa. At a meeting that convenes during the first week of the Gulf War, women talk about their fears and the flashbacks they experience when they hear bombs exploding on television. They wonder if they're in danger of attack, and the American social worker leading the group passes a map around the room, explaining where the Gulf is in relation to the United States and Cambodia (they're worried about relatives too). The war is far away, she assures them. We watch home videos — one tape of the groups' last picnic, another tape of a recent trip back to Cambodia by the groups' Cambodian coleader. She visited a movie set and a movie star — a young woman who adorns a calendar in one of the rooms at the community center — and the women are captivated.

Some meetings are devoted to remembering. Women tell stories about their pasts, before the Khmer Rouge, how they met their husbands, some of whom now are dead or missing. They talk about courtship customs in Cambodia and family life. A Tibetan doctor visits one session and talks about the troubles in his country, and one woman who has lost all her children cries softly. "It is always with us," another woman explains, "especially when we are alone; then, we always remember." She suggests that they gather together partly to forget. "How do you help each other?" the social worker asks. "Sometimes, we tell jokes."

I don't mean to minimize the struggle to begin a new life in a strange, hard country with so little resources and a history of so many losses. I have seen only a moment, barely a moment, in a long passage to recovery. I imagine that many of these women are deeply depressed and may remain so. Some have trouble sleeping and are plagued by bad dreams and need medication to maintain their equilibrium. Still, of all the groups I've visited, these are virtually the only ones that engaged me, the only ones I enjoyed and looked forward to attending, the only ones that left me with a sense of hope.

FIVE

The Recovery Boutique: Workshopping

Marilyn Volker, sex therapist, and codependency expert, is conducting a workshop on "childhood messages about sexuality." Like a talk show host, sleek in purple silk, she works the room, seeking testimony, accosting us with her microphone. When it is my turn, when her microphone is in my face, I politely ask her to move back. Later, when the workshop is over, several women compliment me on my "assertiveness."

John Lee, an acolyte of men's movement guru Robert Bly and author of *The Flying Boy*, a popular codependency book about why men flee from relationships, tells stories about his family, his girlfriends, and his struggles with intimacy. Dressed in jeans and cowboy boots (he's from Texas), with a down-home twang, he confesses his sins against women, playing his all-female audience with the assurance of a middle-aged rock star. After his talk, a parade of women descend on him for autographs and hugs. I ask him if he is ever challenged by an audience. "I don't allow challenges," he says, looking me straight in the eye. "I only accept support."

Yvonne Kay, grief counselor and local radio personality, delivers what is intended as an inspirational, keynote address about her own victory over codependency and low self-esteem. She carries a stuffed swan to the podium to symbolize her metamorphosis and begins her talk by asking members of the audience to stand up and applaud themselves.

Approximately 250 women are gathered here in Philadelphia at the Wyndham Franklin Plaza Hotel for a three-day conference on recovery and self-esteem. In lectures and workshops presented by a roster of codependency/recovery experts, they'll grapple with their addictions to love, food, and other substances, and various forms of abuse; they'll explore their inability to establish boundaries in relationships; they'll ponder the prospect of true intimacy; they'll do some grief work and ferret out their inner children. And they'll buy books by leading recovery experts, some of whom are here in Philadelphia, all of whom are published by Health Communications, Inc., a small, Florida-based recovery publisher and sponsor of this conference.

In 1990, HCI was sponsoring about seventeen or eighteen regional conferences and one national conference every year; it was also venturing out internationally, with conferences in Canada and Australia. Conferences have been aimed at the general, codependent public, which supposedly includes virtually all Americans; but the consuming codependent public appear to be mostly white, female, and middle class. (Out of this group of 250 women in Philadelphia, I see two blacks.) The number of annual conferences and conference attendance has declined since 1990, along with the economy, and the female market for codependency books may have peaked. But there is an emerging market for codependencylike books among men searching for something called "authentic masculinity," and HCI has held an occasional special conference for men. The Philadelphia conference, however, is billed as a women's conference, and in many ways it is like an early exercise in consciousness raising.

The self-professed codependent women here are protesting their passivity, submissiveness, and dependence on men, the ways in which they've been conditioned to put themselves last and endure abuse. It is as if they were discovering what is wrong with femininity for the first time. Consciousness Raising 101. These are women whom feminism bypassed.

But catching up with popular feminism twenty years later, they find a movement diluted by concern for the rights and feelings of men. Men's movement expert John Lee is a featured speaker in the plenary session, opening night. Focusing on men's fear of intimacy, he explains how men have been victimized by a culture that does not allow them to cry. (He has warned us that he won't say much that's new, but it is his presence as much as his insights that the women here crave.) He titillates, with asides about what he says to his girlfriend in bed. He seduces; admitting that he loves women only to leave them, he projects such tentative unavailability. A carefully cultivated cowboy, as rugged as he is sensitive, John Lee seems a man for the '90s, Alan Alda bonded with Clint Eastwood.

Lee calls himself a "flying boy": he flies away from women in perverse attempts to experience emotion: "Getting a woman to leave was one way I could get close to my feelings. . . . But before the grief around that woman was ever expressed, I'd get me another one." Lining up women has never been hard: women love flying boys, Lee confirms. "They chase them, try to catch them and fix them." The audience murmurs appreciatively, and Lee rambles on about himself, his abusive, codependent parents, and his flying boy syndrome in an occasionally coherent collection of one-liners. "You can always spot a flying boy. He's tired of having to flap his wings," he says, and women take notes. He is revealing, I guess, men's anguished, secret lives.

"Flying boys hurt so much inside they can't tell anybody," which is why we need a men's movement, Lee suggests. "Life is not worth living ungrieved." Flying boys are shirking their grief work: "It's hard for flying boys to land because the pain is so bad when they do." Men have an especially hard time dealing with pain because "society had a vested interest in making sure we didn't feel our feelings. I was raised to be unfeeling, angry, to be a killer. . . . Most women don't understand how angry men are," he adds, but, in fact, I think we do.

"It's okay to be angry at anything you want to be angry at," Lee assures us, and women nod. Considering the number of homicides, not to mention rapes, committed each year, I suspect that America suffers from too much anger, not too little; but I am in denial. Unlike guilt and shame, anger is apparently "useful as a way of life" for recovering codependents. Doing "grief work" allows them to "own" their anger, which is part of their entitlement as victims of abuse.

Having experienced, or at least imagined, their own abuse, Lee's audience of recovering women might have been wary of Lee's unqualified validation of anger. Surely they would not agree that it is "okay" to be angry at your child for making demands on you. But in recovery, people seem to think only of their own emotions, which are always justified. You don't hear anyone ask, "If anger is always okay for me, why wasn't it okay for my parents?" Like most codependency experts, Lee wants to help us feel good about ourselves, imbuing us with a sense of our own righteousness. Women have a lot to be angry about too, he informs us.

But women's anger is yesterday's news; Lee is more concerned with the unexamined grievances of men. "As soon as a man gets with a woman he feels some energy moving out of him," he declares in a digression about codependency and men. Men become codependent because "their energy was needed by their mothers," he explains, before catching himself and adding that other family members — siblings or grandparents — can drain men's energy too. Enervated, cut off from their feelings, men retreat into rationalism and "can't readily identify with what they need to grieve about. Men are so much in their heads, as if you didn't know that," Lee says, as if stereotypes of cerebral men and emotional women were indisputably true. "Until recovery kicks in, the grief process is from the neck up."

"Does that make sense to you?" Lee keeps asking rhetorically, but I wonder if sense is what many women here are after. "Men have to fly away because they have to deal with their pain." (Didn't he tell us that men fly away because they *can't* deal with their pain? Never mind.) "Men have to connect with their masculine side . . . most men haven't; they've tried to skirt around and connect with their feminine side." (The macho killers that society trains seem momentarily forgotten; we are now in a world of new, "sensitive" men.) But in "finding the masculine self, men also begin to explore their feminine side." Does that make sense to you?

Lee assures us that the answer is within ourselves: "Most men have to make that journey to find the lover that only lives within. Most women make that journey. The prince lives in the kingdom within. . . . For men, too, the princess is inside, though she's often stone cold dead." It is unclear to me if any of this makes sense to anyone in the audience, but many seem enraptured.

Trust in God is Lee's concluding advice: "Let go and let God be in charge. We're looking for men and women because we haven't got enough of ourselves and we haven't got enough of God." But, in the meantime, "Love for the self or the other comes one day at a time. . . . Love a woman one day because you want to and then you get up the next day and see how you feel."

It is only a little surprising to find the Playboy philosophy, thirty years later, packaged as recovery for men. Plus ça change. (John Lee reminds me that the first great men's movement entrepreneur was Hugh Hefner.) Maybe Lee's endorsement of loving only conditionally, one day at a time, is difficult to reconcile with the recovery movement's heavily promoted ethos of sharing and caring and unconditional love, but this is not a movement that demands, or even recognizes, consistency. Codependency experts borrow haphazardly from popular culture, psychology, and religion. Catch them in a contradiction, and they accuse you of thinking with your head and not your heart.

If ideological confusion is a virtue, codependency experts will be sanctified by their teachings about gender roles. Along with John Lee's veiled misogyny, there are many soft, popular feminist messages about women's need to assert themselves and achieve independence, saying no to abuse and being more than caretakers for their families. Keynote speaker Yvonne Kay opens the conference with a pep talk about empowerment, "putting the focus on yourself . . . learning to love yourself." It is a familiar message, dating back to the beginning of the recovery movement; the process of recovering from codependency has always been billed as a quest for self-love.

Lately, however, codependency experts have been talking about the value of nurturing others as well. Always attuned to cultural trends — today many feminists laud women for sharing and caring more than men — the codependency experts now assure us that they never meant to suggest that women should think only of themselves. *Self-centeredness* (the word, not the phenomenon) is associated with feminism, which is the target of considerable hostility here, despite the uneasiness with traditional notions of femininity. While women complain about having been taught to be selfless domestics, they attack feminism for encouraging them to be selfish careerists.

Jane Middleton-Moz, a popular speaker and author, blames feminism as much as femininity for what's wrong with women today: they're isolated from each other, she says, because feminism taught them to compete. Middleton-Moz chronicles her own disillusionment with both traditional feminine roles and feminism. Unhappy with the notion that women were defined completely by their families, not wanting to become her mother, "an extremely frustrated woman," she found a "new mother" in feminism, until "the new mother became like the critical old mother" she had left behind. Her assumption that most women embraced feminism neurotically, seeking a "new mother," is unquestioned. Now, according to Middleton-Moz, women are assailed by conflicting "do's and don'ts" from the old culture of femininity and the new one of feminism.

She asks the audience to list the old feminine "women-must messages." Women must be submissive and ladylike, they must keep house and never say no, the audience responds. Then they list the feminist "women-must messages." A woman must have a high-powered career, she must always use her head and never her heart, she must be equal to her man.

Perhaps the women here are as threatened by the prospect of equality as they are frustrated by inequality. But whether or not they fear feminism, they misconceive it. They share what has become a prevailing view of feminism, not as a civil rights movement, a movement for social justice, but as a narrow campaign to promote women in corporate hierarchies. During the 1980s, as women doctors, lawyers, and hard-driving executives became fixtures on TV, feminism became identified with yuppieism — an obligatory three-piece suit for women as well as for men. Women must make lots of money, show little compassion, and do no nurturance; that is feminism's primary message, according to Middleton-Moz and her audience. Everyone gets mad at me for suggesting that feminism is a "women-may" and not a "women-must" movement. (Middleton-Moz calls me "madam.") The women here don't associate feminism with choice; they view it as another, harder set of strictures.

This is about as political as a codependency conference gets. Jane Middleton-Moz concludes by announcing that the biggest problem facing women today is "burnout!" If it is striking to hear women talk about what is wrong with femininity without talking about empirical realities such as employment discrimination, the dearth of day care, or domestic violence, it is frightening to see the ease with which people wall themselves up from the world. There is no social or political context here; people talk about themselves as if they were somehow disconnected from society and the nation.

Once again, I irritate Middleton-Moz and her audience when I suggest that women should gaze outward, that burnout may not be our greatest problem after all. What about AIDS, poverty, pollution, sexual and racial violence, not to mention world peace and a few other usual suspects? "You have to work on yourself before you can work on the world," several women quickly retort. Working on both simultaneously is not an apparent option.

That we will reform our dysfunctional society by reforming ourselves and our families is, in fact, the recovery movement's party line. According to John Bradshaw, "the basic problem in the world today is soul-murder," which does sound a bit more problematic than burnout. (If there is ever a battle of the experts, it will be a battle of hyperbole.) Bradshaw suggests that our social crises reflect the fact that adult children are running the world — "our schools, our churches, our government." Recovery will save us as a society, he suggests, somehow staving off totalitarianism and other evils. Some nineteenth-century evangelists professed a similar belief that social reform would be the inevitable result of individual conversions. It is an appealing doctrine, since it saves you the trouble of ever taking action in the world. You have only to recover and the world recovers with you. The primary moral imperative here in Philadelphia, City of Love, is learning to love yourself.

Loving yourself will stop you from losing yourself in relationships, love addiction expert Joy Miller confirms in a workshop on addictive relationships. "Loss of self" in a relationship is "an issue that talks about our basic core," she says tautologically but with an air of genuine concern. One woman in the audience suggests that "victimizing" relationships are mostly "core" issues for women, adding that men would never tolerate the abuse they inflict on women. But the audience generally disagrees. "She can't speak for men," someone calls out, with considerable support. Again, no one offers a factual context; no one mentions that battered spouses and adult victims of other sex crimes are usually women. Miller only points out that "emotional, sexual, and physical abuse are all rape of the soul," and women nod. It is an article of faith here that all suffering is relative; no one says she'd rather be raped metaphorically than in fact.

The crimes in codependency are often metaphoric, like "soul-murder." The goal is to make the self inviolate. Joy Miller wants to help us set "boundaries" and get in touch with our rights. She asks us to divide into groups and devise lists of ten basic relationship rights; people happily comply. After ten or fifteen minutes of conferencing, someone from each group steps up to the mike and reads us our rights. They include: the right to be whatever I want, to be myself and get my needs met; the right to separate, to choose my actions; the right not to be hit; the right not to have to explain myself; the right to my own space; the right to change my mind, to use my brain and grow; the right to follow my bliss.

Miller comments on none of these rights; she only gestures or voices approval of them all. I wonder about a few of them. The right not to explain yourself? What if you don't always make yourself clear? The right to get all your needs met, in one relationship? I wonder how anyone exercising all these rights could ever be in a relationship at all. But around me women are sobbing and hugging and feeling affirmed.

Miller is an effective facilitator — perky, effusive, and earnest, I think, in her efforts to empower us. In another, smaller workshop on love addictions (attributed to failures of self-love), Miller offers to help us "claim our power." She asks us about our affirmations and shares her own: "I am enough. I am whole. I am now."

She instructs us to think of an affirmation, close our eyes, and repeat it ten times to ourselves. Then she suggests that we each find a partner and tell her our affirmation so that she can repeat it back to us. "You are lovable, wonderful, enough," women are telling each other, ten times. People seem to like this exercise, and Miller leaves five or ten minutes for it, filling in with comments: "I'm noting some strong emotion here. I always get excited when I see people cry. Each tear brings us closer to recovery. Cherish each tear."

She wants us to share our feelings about the affirmation exercise. One woman says she couldn't "receive." Hearing her affirmation from her partner didn't mean much because "she doesn't know me." Miller exclaims that this is a typical codependent response, indicative of low self-esteem, an inability to believe someone else can find you lovable. Everything here is a symptom. I can't help suggesting that it may be perfectly rational not to believe a total stranger who says she loves you; maybe resistance to flattery reflects high self-esteem. Later, Miller thanks me for sharing.

She concludes the workshop by having people write love letters to themselves, or, rather, to their inner children. After ten minutes or so of silent writing, people share their letters, reading them out loud to the group. Women are crying, reading letters to their inner kids, like this: "Dear Honeybunch, I love your wide-eyed innocence. I have to get to know you better." Or "Sweetheart, I am very happy that I have begun to know you. You have been lost to me for such a long time. I'm looking forward to your teaching me how to play." A few use the language of romance novels: "Your passion sets me on fire," they say to themselves.

Miller is moved. "There is a lot of hope in here. There are a lot of inner children coming out today," she confirms, hugging almost everyone. One woman who wanders in during the reading of the letters turns to me and says, "This was good, wasn't it?"

Workshops like this are at the heart of the conference and clarify women's reasons for attending, at considerable cost. Conference registration fees are about $200; travel and accommodations can cost hundreds more, and once they arrive, women are bombarded with HCI books as well as tapes of the lectures and workshops they've paid to attend but are forbidden to tape themselves.

Maybe most of the women here don't mind being taped for commercial purposes, and maybe they don't feel exploited. They attend conferences or buy books and tapes only by choice, and many no doubt feel enriched or at least supported by the experience. A conference is an expensive investment for what does not appear to be an upscale crowd — most of the women seem modestly middle-class — but they appear to be satisfied consumers. Maybe there's nothing unethical about HCI conducting business in any manner the market will bear. It's just that the

women here seem so needy and the conference organizers are
so slick.

Still, I suspect that for many women a weekend recovery conference is a little like a weekend at a spa. They come for the
experience of being here, to get their books signed, and to hug
recovery movement celebrities and each other. Reciting affirmations, they get massaged.

I doubt that many women attend to learn anything new
about codependency. I asked a number of women if they heard
anything new, and no one said, "Yes." Several added, however,
that it was "affirming" to hear experts say in person what they
write in their books. Virtually all the information about codependency presented here is readily and much more cheaply
available in books or on tapes, but information is generally
regarded as "too academic" anyway, and there's not much
apparent interest in it. "I don't do facts," John Lee tells us.
"What I want to share with you is not a whole lot of facts."
Instead, he shares stories about his life. Either you "feel" what
he means, "or you don't," he shrugs. But he does offer at least
one "fact": "One of the most major things happening in this
country today is women committing crimes," he claims, apropos
of nothing much, and, as usual, women in the audience nod.

Since there is so little new information presented here, nor
any hard information at all, the content of each presentation
is often the personality of the presenter. This is especially clear
during the first evening of four one-hour lectures, which are
more like performances. (Marilyn Volker tells us we are "walking the line between love and desire and looking for love in-
between," and I expect her to break into song.) Being here is
like being at a floor show or in the audience of a TV talk show
or a televangelist revival. The speakers, celebrities on the
recovery circuit, are all quite slick, and it's clear that they've
given their talks many times: they each speak fluently for an

hour without notes. The audience is starry-eyed, nodding and murmuring throughout.

In nearly three days of lectures and workshops, I am the only person I hear question or challenge an expert. I always take them by surprise, and the audience is always irritated with me. So while the experts routinely disclaim expertise (they often say they are experts only about themselves), they seem to expect their authority never to be questioned, and it virtually never is. The experts hold forth, for a fee, and the audience receives, at a cost.

Yet one of the selling points of the recovery movement is its aggressively egalitarian posture; in keeping with the AA tradition from which it grew, this is supposed to be a leaderless movement of equals. There is no führer — no Werner Erhard, no Reverend Moon, no L. Ron Hubbard. Some experts, like John Bradshaw, are better known and more widely read than others, but the recovery movement is not centered around a single expert any more than Hollywood revolves around a single star.

Experts are required, in fact, to identify with the group, telling us at least a little about their own codependent disorders, and some of the expert confessions are as intimate in subject as the heartfelt cries of the rank and file. On the first night in Philadelphia, Marilyn Volker reveals to an audience of 250 women that her first marriage was not consummated on her wedding night: she had vaginismus and her husband couldn't get it up. It's clear that she has shared this story with many other strangers, many times from many stages. I don't imagine that she's talking to me, but her revelation seems designed to make me feel that I can talk to her. Confessions are routinely used to make the experts seem like common folk, which probably boosts sales, especially for women. One of the most popular women experts, Melody Beattie, is also one of the most approachable (in print, at least; I haven't seen her perform), because her expertise comes almost entirely from her personal experience with addiction. On some level the promise of this movement may be the prospect of celebrity. Anyone who survives codependency and can use a word processor can hope to write a best-selling book.

But the recovery movement is about as truly egalitarian as any established church. If everyone is equal before God or a support group, the shepherds still have more authority than the flock. Behind their silks, makeup, and microphones, the leading women experts in Philadelphia often seem untouchable, while some of the women consumers look like they'd love to be touched by John Lee. Lee, subject of so much feminine adoration, tells me that he doesn't pretend to be an expert, although he is introduced with a string of credentials. He points out that he always tells his audiences that they are free to discard anything he says, but he prospers from their willingness not to. If people regard him as an expert, "that's their problem," he declares, and, I suppose, his reward.

There are, however, at least a few experts in the audience who have paid their way here. Professionals get continuing education credits (CEUs) for attending these conferences, which is a little like getting CEUs for watching "Oprah." Of course, some may simply register and go home. I met one man from New York who showed up briefly for the first day and the last, without missing much. If this is how therapists are being trained, clients are in more trouble than they know.

SIX

Stop Making Sense: New Age

"Talking to a disembodied spiritual entity, even on the telephone, was no longer novel to me," other-world-weary Shirley MacLaine confides, in *It's All in the Playing*, after hanging up on Lazaris. No wonder. Lazaris, an entity helping Shirley with her miniseries (he's channeled through a San Francisco trance medium) has no novel advice, no new wisdom to offer. Talking about the power of unconscious fears and the way you "create your own reality," he speaks the pedestrian language of an ordinary, embodied, talk show therapist.[1]

Most spirits these days seem a bit more arcane, if not incomprehensible; they express themselves best nonverbally. Their provenance, after all, as my friend Barbara reminds me, is a "place where there are no words" — a place like California, where Barbara meditates, makes films, and does her inner child work. "No one here reads anymore," this former English major assures me, "except for a few professors." There are better, nonrational, nonlinear ways of knowing, she suggests, because there are "levels of beingness" that cannot be captured in words.

Still, at the portals of a New Age, undeterred by the limitations of our linear, left-brain language, self-actualizers for whom there are no words persist in writing books. They share their transformative experiences, predict paradigmatic consciousness shifts and new sense modalities, describe processes of spiritual synchronicity, prescribe personal empowerment affirmations, and devise road maps for readers on their own personal odysseys toward the light, the harmonious inner space of self-actualized energy.

You know what they mean. New Age is an attitude. To demand precision and specificity (what some would call meaning) in a discussion of consciousness paradigms or transpersonal energy vibrations is to reveal yourself as only "half-minded," a sorry left-brained creature trapped in rationalism, foolishly focused on the external world. It is to absent yourself from the postbiological, postverbal phase of human evolution and to dwell spiritually in nonlivingness. New Age is aggressively anti-intellectual, proudly nonrational. It's not supposed to make sense. You don't read a book about spiritual odysseys; you experience or process it.

Yet the polysyllabic jargon is deceptive; it sounds as if it ought to be meaningful. A paradigmatic consciousness shift sounds important, even profound. *Paradigm* has long been a favorite word of academics, who discourse about such things as doctrinal paradigms, by which I think they sort of mean ideas, important ideas. More recently, *paradigm* has been discovered by public policy experts seeking new empowerment paradigms, and it has even become a sobriquet: Governor Bill Clinton of Arkansas is a "paradigm liberal," according to political columnist Joe Klein. *Paradigm* has also entered the lexicon of how-to-succeed authors: In his best-selling *The Seven Habits of Highly Effective People*, Stephen Covey rhapsodizes about the "power of a paradigm" and encourages readers to make "paradigm shifts" (the power of a paradigm shift is "the essential power of quantum change").[2]

So, what, if anything, does this versatile word *paradigm* mean? A paradigm is a fundamental concept or model, but, as *Webster's* notes, the word can signify a big, "overall" concept that explains a set of data or processes, which makes it a perfect New Age word — spiritual awakenings and consciousness shifts, like recovery, are always processes, never events.

The phrase "paradigmatic consciousness shift" is, then, a little redundant, but only to a reader who stops to think, a reader who hasn't yet had her consciousness shifted so that she's able to read nonrationally. What is the consciousness shift that awaits her? It seems to be a cerebral movement toward the right, a shift from left- to right-brain sense modalities, which makes it a paradigm that cannot be comprehended by a stubborn, left-brain analysis like this.

Nor can I be sure about spiritual synchronicity, but it is probably what people mean when they talk about being "in sync," which sounds appealing. Since synchronicity means everything happening at once, spiritual synchronicity must have something to do with spiritual oneness, a New Age ideal, or paradigm. (I am you and you are me and we are one together.) Spiritual synchronicity is probably a transformative experience, or a paradigmatic change. *Transformative* is another word New Age shares with the academy. (Jargon seems to be the place where right and left brains meet.) Feminist legal scholars, for example, construct transformative jurisprudential analyses (after they've deconstructed traditional legal theory), while New Age feminists visualize transformative cognitive reconstructions of the masculine mode.

Oh, Goddess. People from the place of no words speak in pretty generalities that are supposed to mean everything — about wisdom, serenity, and spiritual wholeness — instead of nothing. They've devised a language of "inclusivity," having discovered on the way to the marketplace that words only limit when they specify.

New Age writers, however, are carrying on a venerable tradition of not making sense. Theirs is hardly the first movement built on language that is inimical to reason. Mary Baker Eddy's *Science and Health*, the bible of Christian Science, is sound and fury or, as Mark Twain observed, a collection of "showy incoherencies":

> When you read it you seem to be listening to a lively and aggressive and oracular speech delivered in an unknown tongue, a speech whose spirit you get but not the particulars ... you seem to be listening to a vigorous instrument which is making a noise which it thinks is a tune, but which, to persons not members of the band, is only the martial tooting of a trombone, and merely stirs the soul through noise, but does not convey a meaning.[3]

But, like most popular religious and personal development authors, Eddy knew how to create the appearance of meaning, Twain conceded:

> Whenever she notices that she is chortling along without saying anything, she pulls up with a sudden "God is all over us," or some other sounding irrelevancy, and for the moment it seems to light up the whole district; then, before you can recover from the shock, she goes flittingly pleasantly and meaninglessly along again, and you hurry hopefully after her, thinking you are going to get something this time.... Whenever she discovers that she is getting pretty disconnected, she couples up with an ostentatious "But," which has nothing to do with anything that went before or is to come after, then she hitches up some empties to the train — unrelated verses from the Bible, usually — and steams out of sight and leaves you wondering how she did that clever thing.[4]

Politicians and their ghostwriters could learn much from Eddy, or perhaps they already have. Political people instinctively recognize the value of lofty, meaningless phrases: everyone who's afraid of the dark can feel good about a thousand points of light. Political language is a language of euphemism and indirection that has long been a refuge for scoundrels, George Orwell observed. Words like *fascism* and *democracy* are regularly abused by politicians who resist defining their terms. But sometimes even voters seem less starry-eyed than people who long to be self-actualized. Conversant in New Age jargon, they talk about channeling their energy systems, finding their focal awareness points, and engaging in processes of spiritual psychosynthesis with such conviction. Perhaps they know what they mean. A term like "creative beingness" is a Rorschach test: everything you see in it is true.

An all-inclusive jargon is a moral as well as commercial imperative in the New Age because truth is all-inclusive. (I Am the Walrus. We Are the World.) Ways to the truth vary, however, since people are at varying stages of spiritual evolution. Under the umbrella of a vaguely articulated ideal of wholeness, New Age offers a pluralistic collection of techniques to help you achieve it.

There are as many techniques, and variations on jargon, as there are spiritual paths as there are shelves in a New Age bookstore. Between angel directories and recipes for tofu meatloaf, many spirits speak. Some promise to help you harness your power to heal and reclaim the primordial child within, sounding just like twelve steppers who've read a bit too much Jung. Switching channels, others offer access to new, interplanetary dimensions of illumined selfhood, sounding more like fans at a Star Trek convention.

The New Age is an age of choices. You can seek your truth or inner space in a relatively conventional array of Western and Eastern religious literature, in psychology, recovery, and holistic health books, the always intriguing "esoterica," or in astrology, divinations, and revealed teachings. If you're anxious to transcend the material world quickly, read *How to Have an Out-of-Body Experience in Thirty Days* (by the author of *Inner Sex in Thirty Days*). If your path in this life is a material one, you can use your spiritual energies to create wealth (as Napoleon Hill suggested over fifty years ago in *Think and Grow Rich*). *Do What You Love, The Money Will Follow*, one recent bestseller, described by the guy at the bookstore as "yuppie New Age," proclaims. Or you can study *The Seven Habits of Highly Effective People*.

Actually *The Seven Habits* might not appear in every New Age bookstore, and its author, Stephen Covey, who assures us of his belief in "God, the creator and Father of us all," might protest his inclusion in New Age. New Age gurus might be happy to disown him. The spirit of the New Age is not patriarchal: witches, goddesses, buddhas, angels, and spiritual entities of no discernible gender happily cohabit the interstellar space that is New Age. But the best-selling *Seven Habits of Highly Effective People* glows with the aura of New Age; as the book jacket says, it is "holistic." Covey has an ear for grandly meaningless, vaguely spiritual phrases: "The being/seeing change is an upward process — being changing seeing, which in turn changes being, and so forth," he writes, with the air of someone imparting information.[5] By teaching us the Seven Habits, he will help us "break through to new levels of personal and interpersonal effectiveness as we break with old paradigms that may have been a source of pseudo-security." And what are the Seven Habits?

> In harmony with the natural laws of growth, they provide an incremental, sequential, highly integrated approach to the development of personal and interpersonal effectiveness.... They become the basis of a person's character, creating an empowering center of

correct maps from which an individual can effectively solve problems, maximize opportunities, and continually learn and integrate
other principles in an upward spiral of growth.[6]

I doubt that many readers know what this means (I don't),
but they know how it makes them feel. Covey seduces them
with all the right buzzwords: harmony, integrate, interpersonal,
maximize, effectiveness, empowering (eventually he gets around
to synergy). His peroration, the "upward spiral of growth" (a
phrase he repeats often), is uplifting, if you don't mind feeling
like a corkscrew. Covey has a useful talent for saying nothing
inspiringly; he should write commencement speeches.

Not that his talents are wasted. An M.B.A. and chairman
of something called the Institute of Principle Centered Leadership, Covey seems to be a sort of management consultant. His
book may spiral your spirits upward, but it is grounded in
pragmatic concerns about personal and organizational produc-
tivity. The Seven Habits themselves, like most self-help principles, paradigms, and revelations, are essentially a series of
maxims you already know: take initiative, have a goal, set pri-
orities. Covey offers advice about such earthly matters as time
management, human resource management, organizational PC
(production capabilities, not political correctness); he talks
about delegating responsibility and calls "effective delegating"
a "high leverage activity." *The Seven Habits of Highly Effective
People* is corporate New Age. No wonder we've lost our com-
petitive edge.

That spirits can spiral upward and remain tied to the bottom
line is a singular premise of American capitalism. In America
"selling is a form of ecstasy," financial writer Michael Lewis
has remarked. "God and money have never been . . . far apart."[7]
Today's middle managers who came of age in the 1960s may
be especially susceptible to spiritualized business books, one

New Age publisher speculates hopefully, because of their "youthful infatuation with Eastern philosophy." (Two of the best-selling business books of recent years were ancient Chinese classics: *The Teh Ching* and *The Art of War.*) Mainstream publishers are also making money on modern American treatises on the spiritual side of business. According to one Doubleday editor (who has probably read too many of her books), "Business is becoming more and more anthropomorphic. The New Age did speak of a worship of people, not structures, and so we are seeing authors moving away from an idea of business as a mechanism that exists outside the self."[8]

There is, however, nothing new in this view of business as a religion and form of personal development. It was at the center of the Horatio Alger myth. Money has long satisfied spiritual and psychic needs, while established religions, as well as those on the margins, have readily accommodated themselves to the demands of a commercial culture, lending mercantilism some moral authority: nineteenth-century Protestantism effectively sanctified the growing free enterprise system. New Age religion is especially adaptable to business, given its doctrine of inclusivity: it is more easily defined by what it is not — traditional, patriarchal monotheism — than by what it is — practically everything else, from spiritualism to the "science" of positive thinking.

■   ■   ■

If you want to experience or "process" New Age's heady combination of pseudoscience, religion, and money, visit a session or two of The Forum, the new incarnation of est. I'm not suggesting that you pay for the privilege. Forum seminars are expensive — $625 for four days and one evening's worth of wisdom, but you can visit a couple of sessions for free if you are invited by a paying participant. Participants are encouraged to introduce friends and relatives to The Forum: every guest is a potential recruit.

The philosophy of The Forum is essentially the philosophy of est: No excuses. You are totally responsible for all your successes and failures. You have total control of your life. Or, as Shirley MacLaine's spiritual entity, Lazaris, reminds her, you are your own reality. The Forum's $625 introductory program consists of two weekends and one weeknight of pep talks by the program leader and mild browbeating of participants who testify and complain about their lives. (Forum seminars are much less abusive than est training sessions were, and everyone has free access to bathrooms.) There are no cross conversations between participants; you interact directly only with the leader, who controls the seminars totally, as you are supposed to control your own life.

This program of testimony and exhortation is familiar enough; the only mystery is why people pay so much money to partake in it. The Forum's promotional literature, however, offers a vague, entirely abstract description of itself that makes a hackneyed program seem grand and arcane:

> The Forum provides a breakthrough to a new dimension of possibility.... The Forum is a powerful, practical inquiry into the issues that determine our personal effectiveness in all facets of our lives. This inquiry demands the courage of adventure.... The breakthrough available in The Forum is produced by examining our most cherished assumptions, and by stepping boldly beyond them. It's a breakthrough that leads to decisive, effective action that shapes a future, advances intentions, achieves our goals, and contributes powerfully to families, communities, and to the world we share.[9]

This is the kind of "inspirational," content-free language we expect to find in a promotional brochure; it's like a MasterCard commercial that commands you to "master the possibilities."

Writing like this is easy; even computers can do it. You need only master the vocabulary — power, practical, breakthrough, decisive, adventure, share, community. In The Forum, people talk like this too. At the session I attend, the leader, a talking Ken doll, proclaims that The Forum will teach us "to access new dimensions of being." His language is a fluent hybrid of computerese (he is always accessing and interfacing), bureaucratese (his syntax is quite contorted), and New Age psychobabble.

"One of the major distinctions of The Forum that we impact is that we focus on living, not knowing," he declares. But despite this disdain for knowing, The Forum is concerned with learning, offering a special learning technique: "This method of learning is what we call distinguishing," the leader explains. Its goal is "learning to function by insight, instead of building information." (Or, as codependency experts say, think with your heart and not your head.) There are "different fields of study," he informs us: "The field in which we study in The Forum is living — how to live effectively — how to manage the experience of being alive. Life is a privilege. . . . The Forum accesses a new dimension of yourself as a human being. It's what you don't know and don't know that you don't know."

Oh, do not ask what is it. Let us go and make our visit.

■   ■   ■

There are about 250 to 300 people participating in the session I attend (representing, according to my calculations, as much as $187,000 to The Forum).* We are seated in rows, lecture style;

*I'm figuring 300 people at $625 a head. It is worth noting that these $625 introductory programs are apparently conducted regularly throughout the nation: in my region, according to the leader of our session, there were three or four programs offered during about a two-month period. In addition, The Forum offers a Six-Day Advanced Course for $1,300 (you can review this six-day course for a mere $750). It offers courses for children and teens and a long list of courses or seminars in selected topics, such as transformation, communication, and empowerment. This appears to be a multi-million-dollar business that produces nothing but rhetoric.

the leader is miked. He introduces the session by telling us about the wonderful breakthroughs people have achieved through The Forum's unique, dynamic program in self-knowledge, discovery, and effectiveness that holds the key to authentically experiencing life. He is primarily addressing the invited guests, whom he hopes to recruit. Through The Forum we will explore our individuality, learn how to activate vital relationships, effectively communicate, and fully experience being. "We look at ways of being able to contribute. We look at the phenomenon called peace of mind. As you hear people sharing, you'll hear people talk about how this has impacted their way of life."

That, of course, is a cue for people to share, and some do. A series of people stand up, each to considerable applause, and testify. "The Forum opened up a new place for me to start from in my relationships. It changed my consciousness about how I perceived other people," a young man says. "It makes the way you are within yourself better." (In one or two Forum sessions, you can learn to speak like this too.) The leader comments on each piece of testimony; or rather, he repeats his comments about accessing new dimensions, learning to live effectively and by instinct: "What you know has nothing to do with the way you live. From a two-dimensional reality you will never get a sphere. The Forum brings an added dimension to what you have in your life right now. We call this — dimension possibility!"

In forty-five minutes or so — I lose track — the leader hardly ever actually says anything. But borrowing some language from technology, he borrows the appearance of precision, and he tirelessly repeats key words and phrases — effectiveness, new dimensions of being, accessing, systems, authentic, commitment, totality. The effect is a little hypnotic, and most people in the room gazing at him seem impressed. "That man over there changed my life," one man testifies, pointing to the leader. "Coming to The Forum gave me love, happiness, and the possibility for a relationship. I owe this guy my life." A woman testifies that a few days of Forum sessions "changed twenty-eight years of how I related to my father."

The leader explains how The Forum effects these miraculous changes so quickly. It offers "positive reinforcement to people willing to open themselves to the experience." The only people who will fail to benefit from The Forum are "people who dismiss it by saying they know it all," he adds, in case we were thinking of not signing up.

After an hour or so of testimony and harangues by the leader, the guests are split up into two groups — one group of people interested in joining The Forum themselves, another (my) group that would simply like to hear more "information" about Forum programs.

I join about thirty people in a small room, where two female apprentice leaders assure us that The Forum is the place to "discover and unleash potential, to tap into yourself, getting knowledge or experience." Several times I ask them to describe the program a little more concretely. "What happens in a seminar? What do you actually do?" Several times they respond, "The Forum experience cannot be described. It can only be experienced." They remind me that "The Forum results go beyond the moment of insight, and life is too important for you to be less than you can be. The Forum provides opportunities for meeting demands." Then we watch a promotional video consisting of testimony by high achievers: an Olympic athlete, actor Raul Julia, and a handsome, wealthy businessman living with his handsome family in the Swiss Alps all tell us that The Forum changed their lives and made them what they are today.

After this exchange of information, the larger group reunites for a concluding, plenary session. We are back in the room with the leader, who is making his final pitch. "When I'm around people who are committed, it's inspiring to me," he confides. More people testify: "There is a final yes after every no," one man says. Another pays tribute to the leader: "I feel I got a piece of a mirror from you. And I like what I see." The leader pays tribute to the group: "I see in you a commitment to fulfilling the potential of what life can be on the planet, fulfilling what you are committed to. What gets me up in the morning is sharing what you share." Finally the leader pays tribute to The Forum: "Martin Luther King and John Kennedy made it happen." The Forum, "this technology," can make it happen too.

This technology? The Forum is carefully packaged as a science, not an art. In a high-tech age in which computers are literally child's play, science enjoys considerable cachet, despite a renewed interest in spirituality. New Age appropriates science, or tries to, in an effort to bolster its credibility and expand its market. New Age embraces pop neuroscience — the science of speculations about the creative ("feminine") right side of the brain and the analytic ("masculine") left side, the science of brain wave machines that offer push-button Nirvana. Having trouble meditating, peaking, or exploring the furthest reaches of human consciousness? At an altered-mind-states gym, in Cambridge or L.A., you can hook yourself up to an Inner Quest 111 or an MC²Dreamachine. The Dreamachine may look like a walkman, but it is really a "training device for people to experience the multidimensionality of their brain waves.... [It] helps you get there effortlessly without the hassle of mantras or lotus positions."[10]

The blend of spiritualism and pseudoscience that you find in an altered-mind-states gym is familiar, dating back at least one hundred years to mind cure and Christian Science. It is a powerful and profitable blend, as Mary Baker Eddy, Norman Vincent Peale, and Napoleon Hill demonstrated. Packaged as science, any wishes, speculations, and the wackiest "systems" for success and salvation are transformed, through the alchemy of the marketplace, into established, objective truths.

The truths may make no sense, but that only proves their validity. "Embrace the mystery," New Age enthusiasts would say. You're not supposed to analyze the truth or process it logically; in the New Age, you're not required to pay attention. Even the words of best-selling authors only signify outer realities. They outline the techniques that lead you to a self-actualized perceptual space of inner silence, just as brain wave machines take you to a place of hemispheric synchronization, where your brain is in a state of oneness and, at last, there are no words.

That a disdain for rationalism can comfortably coexist with an attraction to science is one of the wonders of personal development in America. It is also one of the benefits of irrationalism; experts on spirituality and selfhood revel in their inconsistencies. But if the appropriation of science by self-styled spiritual leaders reflects some underlying ideological confusion, it does make sense commercially; that is, it makes money.

By laying claim to science, New Age entrepreneurs hope to lay claim to a share of the science market. Publishers are avoiding the term New Age, *Publishers Weekly* recently reported, and seeking new, more credible, "scientific" labels for their books, like "New Paradigms." Bantam, a leading New Age publisher, has launched a New Science imprint, "hoping to capture the market that has been buying Stephen Hawking's *A Brief History of Time* and James Glieck's *Chaos* in droves."[11] Bantam is also limiting its use of the New Age label because it alienates readers who associate New Age with crystals, channeling, and other marginal spiritual pursuits. But only the label is changing, not the books or the motto of Bantam's spiritual line, "A Search for Meaning, Growth, and Change."[12] Who would dare scorn that?

New Age books aren't disappearing so much as dissolving into the mainstream, *Publishers Weekly* suggests. As New Age publisher Jeremy Tarcher notes, "We do books on child rearing, personal health, business, Jungian psychoanalysis, men's consciousness, sexuality, and all are now subjects one can look at with a New Age perspective."[13] And, if channeling and crystals are a little passé, an interest in tarot cards persists. So does belief in the Goddess or Cosmic Mother of us all. Over 100,000 people are said to worship Her nationwide. Goddess books, or "feminist spirituality" books, have not yet been over-published, according to one publisher in the field, and of course books about male spirituality constitute the newest and most promising New Age/personal development craze, led by Robert Bly (with a little help from Bill Moyers).[14] "Men's consciousness" books now have their own shelf in my neighborhood bookstore, next to women's books, psychology, and recovery.

Iron John, Robert Bly's recent best-seller that started this lucrative trend, crosses several publishing categories. It combines codependency theory (references to addiction and abuse) with antifeminism (complaints about emasculating women) with popular mythology (in the style of Joseph Campbell, Moyers's other contribution to the culture) and popular, reductionist history. (The industrial revolution separated fathers from their sons, Bly laments, without a footnote or any other substantiation, of course. I guess he's never heard of the postindustrial, bourgeois family business.) But most of all, *Iron John* bears the hallmark of New Age — it is portentous and vaguely spiritual, and it rarely makes sense. You can glean from it attitudes — male bonding is good, feminism is bad, self-absorption is a spiritual virtue — but you may be unable to specify the book's ideas. It has the elusiveness of advertising copy that makes you feel good without conveying any information, like this excerpt from the publisher's promotional blurb:

> *Iron John* is at the same time a new vision and a very ancient vision
> of adult manhood, one that has depth, vividness, and solidity. It
> reconfirms the power of ancient stories to guide, to heal, and to
> convey the deepest truths.[15]

You know what this means — nothing — still, it sounds important, like most of this book. Bly writes about "Zeus energy" and the "wounds" to "our princehood," and the "genuine patriarchy [that] brings down the sun through the Sacred King"; he ponderously offers allegories of male initiation rites and tributes to the Wild Man: "what the psyche is asking for now is a new figure, a religious figure but a hairy one, in touch with God and sexuality, with spirit and earth." He substitutes sanctimony for sense, and soon grown men are off in the woods, crying, chanting, and beating their drums.[16]

Personal development, popular spirituality, and consciousness raising movements have been targeting women for so long; it is gratifying to see that the sexes are equally silly. Like the recovery movement, The Forum, some branches of feminism, and all of New Age, the men's consciousness movement celebrates feeling at the expense of rationality. The trouble with men is that they are "numb from the neck down," men's movement converts regularly assert. As one New Man explained to a *Boston Globe* reporter, "one problem I've always had as a man was intellectualizing everything, always analyzing and justifying, never experiencing much at a feeling level. Then I went into a Bly workshop that got me out of my head and into my gut."[17]

If you want to denigrate thinking, call it intellectualizing. If you want to elevate thoughtlessness, call it experiencing at a feeling level. Talk about body and spirit consciousness and feeling realities — deeper truths than our minds can comprehend — if you want to sound enlightened and redeemable.

New Age promises to take us beyond language and reason itself: in nonsense lies salvation. Linear, logical, left-brain analytic (male-identified) thinking is blamed for every ill from war to pollution to poverty and serial murders, in the literature of New Age as well as recovery. Language is part of our problem — it's a mental exercise, not a spiritual one. Intellectuals are dinosaurs. We're evolving nonverbally, following our bliss to a new, nonrational age. (I thought we were already there.)

Listening to the weird New Age babble of bliss-speak, techno-talk, and personal development proverbs, while the experts bemoan the excessive rationality of our culture, I wonder. Am I the only person who thinks we've gone crazy? Assaulted by sound bites and slogans that pass for political discourse, gossip that passes for news, and anecdotes that take the place of ideas, I never feel surrounded by rationality. My idea of heaven is a rational world; but I must have blinked during our literate, intellectual phase (it must have flashed by in a video), because here we are in some postliterate, postintellectual space, in which language is supposed to convey only an attitude, and a word means no more than a smile.

SEVEN

God Is a Good Parent Too: Self-Help and Popular Theology

New Age spiritualism is an affront to traditional monotheism — some conservative religious sects consider it Satanism
— but it is securely placed in the motley American spiritual
tradition that embraces mind cure, New Thought, and positive
thinking. Atheism is what's considered un-American. As any
child of the cold war knows, atheism and communism are inex-
tricably bound; so were Americanism and Protestantism one
hundred years ago. This is a Christian, or Judaeo-Christian,
or deeply spiritual country, pundits and politicians regularly
proclaim. Under the rubric of religious freedom, we respect the
right to worship differently much more than the right to worship not at all.

Intolerance of disbelief is a subtext of most popular, prescriptive religious literature. If not condemned, nonbelievers are
pitied and patronized. If not considered sinful, atheism is
mourned as a corrosive, self-defeating dysfunction. Of course,
religious writers who lack conviction that they offer a better
way would hardly be religious at all (or maybe they wouldn't

be writers). Their certainty of belief is worth noting, however, because of its importance as a marketing tool, because of the place their books occupy in the publishing business and popular culture. Straddling the secular and sacred, popular religious books are hybrids — using self-help/success primer techniques to instruct, inspire, or indoctrinate religious belief on the grand scale.

No review of the personal development tradition would be complete without a review of popular religious teachings, particularly today. Religion and psychology have always been tied by the common questions about selfhood they address; today they are even offering some common answers. The recovery movement is less secular than nondenominational, and popular religious books are infused with the precepts of popular psychology, as well as the spirit of self-help publishing.

Doubtful self-help authors don't sell many books, sacred or secular. Their readers seek answers, formulas, and guarantees, not inquiry and speculation. The tentative and tortured theologies of William James, Dostoevsky, or Kafka would probably not answer the needs of people who read M. Scott Peck, Harold Kushner, Charles Swindoll, James Dobson, and other popular writers I've reviewed.

Theology may be, in fact, too grand a term for the attitudes and proclamations that popular religious books comprise. These are not, in general, books of argument; they don't engage readers in dialogue and exploration. Instead of reasoning or arguing, they pronounce, admitting no distinctions among opinion, desire, and truth.

This is, in part, an occupational hazard, or perquisite, depending on your point of view. "God loves you" is not a provable or even arguable assertion. But these books are not billed as simple declarations of belief; they are marketed as primers on personality development and psychotherapy, child rearing, spouse abuse, deprivation, and despair, as well as the search for love, happiness, and salvation. Readers who find the answers to existential questions and various social crises less than self-evident should seek their counseling elsewhere.

It seems indisputable, however, that hordes of people do find comfort, and maybe guidance, in these books. M. Scott Peck's first book, *The Road Less Traveled*, spent years on the *New York Times* best-seller list. The market for more specialized Christian writers is thriving too, and Christian books published by religious presses are beginning to enter the mainstream. It would be both futile and presumptuous to deny the benefits experienced by so many readers, whose tastes and ideals I don't share.

As a skeptical, secular humanist, Jewish, feminist, intellectual lawyer, currently residing in the Ivy League, I belong to a number of groups disdained by conservative religious writers, who dominate the field, and I'm probably not the target audience even for the less doctrinaire. Just as codependency authors will dismiss my critique of their efforts by dismissing me as someone "in denial," traditional religious writers, I suspect, will dismiss or pity me as a lost and angry soul; in their eyes I am someone who has not seen the light, or perversely refuses to look at it.

Smugness coupled with false humility is a common, central trait of popular religious writers. They like to quote themselves, clumsily re-creating self-serving conversations with others, citing passages from their earlier books: they are their own authorities. Disclaiming their own greatness, modestly presenting themselves as fellow seekers, fallible and struggling, they carefully repeat the praise they get from others. M. Scott Peck's patients regularly thank him for his insights and compassion, paying tribute. "You really do care for me after all," one woman says, all aglow.[1] "You're one of the few people who has ever understood me," a member of one of Peck's community workshops says, after Peck has summed him up in a paragraph.[2] Christian family counselor and radio personality James Dobson is fond of reprinting testimonial letters he receives from readers and listeners.[3] The generally likable David Seamands, former missionary and pastor turned professor, introduces his first book with the tearful praise he received from one of his mentors: "David, I've never heard a sermon quite like that before. . . . I believe what you have found is the answer."[4] Charles Swindoll, pastor and prolific evangelical writer (who also has a radio show), admits that a man who praises him for his compassion, open-mindedness, and humor has got him "pegged."[5]

The sanctimony is surely heartfelt, but it is also a marketing tool. In order to sell their messages, popular religious writers have to sell themselves. Since there is so little substance to their books — little information, arguments, or new ideas — their power of persuasion is purely personal, deriving from trust in the authorial voice and the portraits they paint of themselves. To feel reassured or enlightened by these books, you have to like the authors and believe in them, trusting in their certitude.

Precisely what are they certain about? Some common attitudes or preoccupations emerge from a sampling of over thirty popular Christian books:

- The universe is essentially a moral, just, and ordered place, in which everything happens for the best or, at least, can be put to good use. Faith illuminates the silver linings; it makes happiness and salvation available to everyone.

- The universe is not a place to navigate alone. Self-sufficiency, or the pretense of it, is a sin. We are not the masters of our fate. We must acknowledge our dependence on God; by submitting to Him we receive His love.*

---

*At the risk of offending some readers, I refer to God as He, because that is what She, He, or It is called by popular religious writers.

- American individualism, "selfism," competitiveness, and the ethic of achievement are sinful too, as well as unhealthy, isolating us from God and each other, focusing our energies on worldly pursuits, fostering the arrogant illusion of self-sufficiency.

- Loving yourself, however, is as important as loving your neighbor; it is the basis for a healthy relationship with God (which is essentially individual, not communal). Loving yourself is even a scriptural imperative: Low self-esteem is sinful, like self-sufficiency. It is an affront to God who loves you, warts and all.

- Evil is a kind of personality disorder, which is not to deny the existence of Satan. Personality disorders may be weapons of Satan; like a bad parent, he deprives you of self-esteem and plays upon your weaknesses.

- God is a good parent, loving and trustworthy, who asks only that you allow Him to redeem you. Salvation is a function of faith.

What is interesting about these familiar messages is their blend of religion, popular psychology, and popular communitarian critiques of American culture. Although many, if not most, religious books are published by religious presses and speak to subcultures of believers, especially conservative Christians, they partake in prevailing mainstream notions about goodness, health, selfhood, and social relations. The boundary between theology and social science has been crossed before, notably by William James, more recently by Joshua Liebman, whose 1948 best-seller, *Peace of Mind*, looked forward to a redemptive collaboration between religion and psychoanalysis. Divinity schools have long offered courses in pastoral counseling. And, on the margins of denominational religion, from New

Thought and Christian Science to New Age, spiritualism has sought credibility in pseudoscience, describing the magic of cosmic energy while borrowing from new theories about the human psyche and the power of imagination. But the marriage of religion and psychology has been tentative and episodic, disrupted by Freud, and marked by periods of considerable hostility on both sides for much of this century. Now, we're witnessing not just a truce but a remarkable accommodation.

Religious writers would minimize or dismiss the effect of psychology on religion, fiercely denying that it has made doctrinal changes, but it does seem to have influenced the tone and packaging of religious appeals. There are few warnings about fire and brimstone and lots of encomiums to mercy and grace. God is invariably portrayed as the ideal parent whose love you can never exhaust; you can only reject it. Do our notions of good parenting derive from our relations with God, as religious writers suggest, or is our vision of God shaped by our parents? How you answer that question probably determines whether at heart you're a cleric or a shrink.

Meanwhile, Christian therapy is a burgeoning field. Like Dolly Parton singing Gershwin, Christian crossovers to psychology combine a kind of pastoral counseling with the practice of individual or family therapy, often focusing on popular problems of addiction and abuse. Christian codependency books, like those produced by the Minirth-Meier clinic in Texas, are practically indistinguishable from codependency books published by secular writers, except for their reliance on Jesus. "The most effective means for overcoming codependent relationships is to establish a relationship with Christ himself," Frank Minirth, cofounder of the Minirth-Meier clinic, writes.[6] David Seamands also draws heavily on popular psychology, stressing that the insights of psychotherapists come from God and that counseling is God's work. M. Scott Peck stresses that mental and spiritual problems are one.

Complementing this embrace of psychology by religious writers is the increasing religiosity of popular psychology. Therapists are urged to heed their clients' spiritual needs (M. Scott Peck is offered as a role model);[7] and twelve-step groups, of course, are covertly religious, invoking higher powers and describing addiction as enthrallment to a false god. For people struggling with addictions and personality disorders, real and imagined, the messages from religion and psychology are compatible and clear: therapy is a door to redemption and faith is a door to recovery.

Religious writers justify their reliance on psychology by praising it for "catching up" to some eternal truths, but they've also found a way to make the temporal truths of psychology palatable. Religious leaders once condemned psychoanalysis for its moral neutrality (Freud made everyone "nice," Fulton Sheen complained).[8] Now popular religious literature equates illness with sin (Satan works through personality disorders), which makes psychology a penitential technique, if not a form of exorcism. Religious writers stress repeatedly that psychology is only a spiritual tool; some therapists might consider religion a therapeutic one. But whether psychology has caught up to religion, infiltrated it, or been adopted by it, the most popular versions of both psychology and religion are becoming less and less distinguishable. Like Macy's and Gimbel's, therapists and religious leaders are happily staking out a common market.

■　　　■　　　■

M. Scott Peck is the most successful, widely known Christian therapist with the broadest mainstream audience. His books turn up on the most unexpected shelves, in the homes of people you'd swear were agnostic. But Peck is in touch with his times. In the past fifteen years, his own career path as an expert and best-selling author has taken him from a generalized, inclusive belief in God to Christianity and from the conduct of individual therapy to workshops in building community, in keeping with cultural trends toward organized religion and the idealization of community.

Peck did not turn to Christianity until after publication of *The Road Less Traveled*, published in 1978. It cloaked a familiar, popularized account of psychotherapy in the vague, nondenominational, Star Wars sort of spirituality that was popular in the late 1970s. Psychotherapy is presented as an act of love. Emotional growth is said to involve acceptance of God. (People "grow in the direction of belief."[9]) Then, in 1980, at the age of forty-three, Peck was baptized, as he reveals in the introduction to his second book, *People of the Lie*, a discussion of evil and demonic possession. ("We must ultimately belong either to God or the Devil," he warns.[10]) His third book, *The Different Drum*, is a paean to community and a description of his own accomplishments as a leader in community building techniques, which draws on Robert Bellah's trend-setting 1985 book, *Habits of the Heart*.

Despite his conversion, Peck is the least doctrinaire of the popular Christian writers and so the most accessible to non-Christians with amorphous spiritual yearnings. The image of God that emerges from his books is a cross between a gentle patriarch and a New Age life force. Although Peck has devoted an entire book to the subject of evil, and occasionally notes that life is hard, he shares the optimism and belief in salvation of most popular Christian writers, and like virtually all self-help writers, he assures readers that everything is possible once you master the right techniques. "With total discipline we can solve all problems," he promises in the opening pages of his first book, and discipline itself is only a "system of techniques." As for evil, it is "strangely ineffective as a social force,"[11] which would surprise anyone who has even heard of genocide. Through Christ, "the defeat of evil is utterly assured,"[12] and "the human race is spiritually progressing. . . . We are growing toward godhead."[13]

"It's like reading a million fortune cookies," I thought about Peck's first book, until I got used to it. Contemplating suffering, redemption, and various existential uncertainties, he is Hamlet played by Polonius.

What is there to analyze in books of platitudes billed as revelations? Sometimes all you can say in response to his assertions is "Oh." We learn that "human beings are profoundly different and profoundly similar,"[14] and "truth is reality. That which is false is unreal." "Ultimately love is everything," he says, paraphrasing the Beatles, promising us that "the mystery of love will be examined in later portions of this work." Indeed, we soon learn that love is the "energy for discipline," which is itself the "means of human spiritual evolution."[15] Oh.

Even Peck's most avid readers would probably have trouble explaining his ideas. Talking about Peck's theology, people often talk simply about Peck: He is loving, wise, patient, firm yet kind, they say, describing the perfect parent (and the God who emerges from most of these books). Or they ruminate very generally about themes and buzzwords that run through most contemporary self-help literature — self-awareness and self-esteem, spiritual growth (or evolution), and the discovery of a loving, omniscient force outside yourself.

Submission to this force — voluntary surrender of the self to God — is, of course, a primary religious impulse, perhaps a basic human one. At least on occasion, everyone wants to let go. Whether that's a measure of holiness or weakness, God knows. The experience of self-surrender is idiosyncratic and probably impossible to apprehend secondhand. Some religious people attest that surrender to God is not bondage but the soul's liberation from the temporal, material world. But respecting the power and passion of their private religious experiences, I still can't help worrying about the public impact of a mandate to submit, which appears in its simplest, most vulgarized form in much popular religious literature as well as in the recovery movement.

If salvation, or recovery, is a struggle, it is a struggle of the will. Peck defines evil as the "unsubmitted will . . . it's almost tempting to think that the problem of evil lies in the will itself. . . . There are only two states of being: submission to God and goodness or the refusal to submit to anything beyond one's own will — which refusal automatically enslaves one to the forces of evil.[16] Ultimately, the only good thing you can will is willingness.

Liberals, romantics, and any student of totalitarianism may find this chilling. There is surely enough recent historical evidence associating submission, not independence of will, with enslavement to evil. In their eagerness to submit, not everyone can distinguish God from the devil.

Popular religious writers tend to address this problem briefly or breezily, or incoherently, if at all. James Dobson, an unabashed authoritarian, is concerned with the problem of permissiveness, not submission. An expert on the family, he seems obsessed with vanquishing rebellious children, asserting that the task of a parent is to "conquer the will."[17] Charles Swindoll concedes that there are "cultic leaders" who take advantage of submissiveness: "*Any* minister who requires blind loyalty and unquestioning obedience is suspect," he says, but that is all he says. "With all that cleared up we are now ready for some positive input into the correct mentality of a servant," he concludes,[18] as if the Holocaust might have been prevented with a homily. M. Scott Peck muses abstractly about the difference between false and true religions, which readers may or may not find helpful: "Truth in religion is characterized by inclusivity and paradox. Falsity [by] onesidedness and failure to integrate the whole."[19]

To true believers, I suppose, the difference between the false and the true is simply self-evident. Supreme Court Justice Potter Stewart's famous remark about obscenity, "I know it when I see it," may be all we can finally say about God. But that isn't saying much in a world in which some die and kill for Allah, some for Christ, and some for ideologies, while others send their savings to Jim Bakker. I'm not suggesting that religious writers are responsible for curing mass hysteria, meanness, bad judgment, and bad faith. But writers regarded as experts on God who preach submission share some of the blame for its consequences.

Swindoll, Dobson, Peck, and others would probably respond that they only lead readers toward what's true (and we can only take their word for that). Or they might deny that they ignore the problem of submissiveness, pointing to the occasional sentence acknowledging it. Peck admits that there is such a thing as "unhealthy nationalism,"[20] but he doesn't blame it on the abdication of will he preaches, to which we owe the Nuremberg defense.

It is, at first, a little surprising to see more rhetoric about submission than individual freedom of action and thought in what are, after all, American self-help books. Religious teachings about submission are, on their face, at odds with the mystique of individualism and the self-willed, self-made man. Individualism is rather out of fashion, and religious writers rail against it, but it is still an important strain of Americanism. To an American audience it would still seem important at least to explain that in voluntary submission to God lies freedom. Fulton Sheen did this eloquently in his best-selling 1949 book, *Peace of Soul:*

> To the extent that we abandon our personality to Him, He will take possession of our will and work in us . . . by almost imperceptible suggestions that rise up from within. . . . He suggests to us; we are never conscious of being under command. Thus our service to Him becomes the highest form of liberty.[21]

Popular religious writers today rarely rise to Sheen's rhetorical heights; literacy and standards for popular writing have declined in the past forty years. But it is also worth noting that Sheen was writing in opposition to emerging postwar personal development movements: *Peace of Soul* is, in some ways, an answer to Joshua Liebman's *Peace of Mind* and a powerful diatribe against psychoanalysis. Not writing from within the tradition he was attacking, (as religious self-help writers partly do), Sheen could explore the nature of submission directly, without subterfuge. His message about submission is complex but clear, undiluted by the rhetoric about doing it your way that is common in self-help literature. Nor does he seem compelled to profess periodically that he has no special insights about God, as self-help writers today are expected to do. That's how they make their authority palatable — how they reconcile the mandate for self-surrender with the quest for self-improvement.

Self-help writers, religious or not, also like to present themselves as mere facilitators of spiritual, personal, or professional development, saying that saving yourself or succeeding is an individual process: everyone has his or her own road to traverse. Self-help generally carries on a tradition of pietism, in some peculiarly mercantile American way. But the individualizing of religious experience, or spiritual journeys, is partial, leaving no one independent of God. Only the process is individualized, not the ultimate truth that the process is aimed at uncovering. There may be many roads but only one destination — the true and only God. Often the experts share in His glory.

Like secular self-help writers, religious ones are rarely honest on the subject of authority and submission. They almost always claim a fellowship with their readers, admitting their own fallacies, sins, and neuroses — Gordon MacDonald devotes a book to his repentance of adultery; M. Scott Peck briefly confesses a character disorder. But disclaiming expertise, self-proclaimed experts can only be liars or frauds. Peck mentions the need to tolerate ambiguity and talks about not leading, but he always sounds quite sure of himself, and he's marketed as a leader and a seer. He bemoans our tendency to "let our authorities do our thinking for us,"[22] but it's a tendency on which he thrives.

That Peck views himself as an authority to whom others should submit is clear in his descriptions of encounters with individual patients and groups involved in community building. People who challenge him are generally presented as evil or, at best, spiritually unevolved; in any case they're always wrong. A psychologist who drops out of one of his community building workshops, claiming that a group of nearly sixty people cannot become a community in two days, apparently gets her come-uppance: after she leaves, "the remaining 58 of us became a community," Peck reports, another claim we can take only on faith. People who "slip away" from his workshops once community has been formed perhaps "just cannot bear that much love," Peck muses.[23] People who do not share his vision of community and disrupt his groups are "evil"; virtually his only reported failure in community building is blamed on an evil woman member who can match his power and "gain[ed] enough allies against me to polarize the group and keep it that way."[24] Somehow I long to hear her side of it.

I wonder about his individual therapeutic failures too, as well as his successes. Practically the only patients he can't help seem to be the ones who willfully reject his wise authority.

It's not exactly that Peck is never wrong; it's just that he seems to err only on the side of goodness, believing people can be better than they are.

His case studies are hard to believe, partly because his re-creation of dialogue is so clumsy. (He has no ear; everyone sounds alike.) Case studies are routinely fictionalized; maybe we're not meant to take them literally. Peck's cases are pat, self-serving little moral tales that often end with his startlingly incisive diagnosis: he likes telling patients "face to face what [he] thinks of [them]," which rarely takes more than a paragraph. By revealing his "positive feelings" for one patient, he cures her of promiscuity and leads her to a happy life: "From among her dozens of lovers Marcia immediately picked one and established a meaningful relationship with him which eventually led to a highly successful and satisfying marriage."[25]

Lucky Marcia. Charlene is a more interesting figure, perhaps the most interesting of Peck's patients — the archetypal evil one who will not be redeemed. She is dishonest, withholding information "for no other reason than to keep control of the show." (Maybe she didn't trust him.) She is also sexually aggressive, not just haplessly promiscuous like Marcia; she comes on to him, and he is repelled, "nauseated," which is a clue to her malevolence. "Certainly I usually have no difficulty feeling warmly toward patients who entrust their love to me," Peck assures us.[26]

Peck presents Charlene as quite sick (he later discovers she's bad) and works with her for nearly four years. She does not progress; indeed at one point she rejects God, crying out that she does not want to live for Him. What further proof have we of Charlene's evil? How does he "sum up" the "alien" force in her? Well, there's her attitude toward the weather. Charlene only liked "grey days . . . dismal days," either because "they made the rest of us miserable," Peck suggests, or because "she love[d] them for their ugliness and vibrate[d] to something in them so utterly alien that we have no name for it."[27] Maybe she was simply depressed.

Despite her perversity, Peck is patient and compassionate, it seems, as usual. Charlene's ultimate failure as a patient is just that — her failure, not his. She leaves uncured mainly because of "her failure to regress," to become a child with him, innocent and truly trusting.[28]

Unless you trust Peck absolutely, it is impossible to know whether Charlene was evil and incurable. It does seem likely that their relationship, if it existed, was fraught with power plays. What he apparently disliked most about her, apart from sexual aggressiveness, was her willfulness and desire for control: "Charlene's desire to make a conquest of me, to toy with me, to utterly control our relationship, knew no bounds." And she does enjoy a "petty" victory over him in the end, terminating the relationship over his objections in a "remarkable tour de force."[29]

Charlene's case is worth describing not just because Peck takes so much time with it, but because as a depiction of evil, she is so predictable; that is, she is what you would expect Peck to choose as an embodiment of evil — a sexually aggressive, controlling female patient who challenges his authority and will not play the child to his perfect parent. Peck's most memorable evil characters are stereotypically evil women; apart from Charlene there are a dreadful dominatrix and a couple of selfish, narcissistic mothers. Peck suggests in passing that bad mothers cause schizophrenia: "I frequently found the mothers of schizophrenics to be extraordinarily narcissistic individuals."[30] Readers aware of evidence that schizophrenia is an inheritable disease may question Peck's motives and judgment. But maybe they can't bear that much love.

For some people even loving psychotherapy is not redemptive (in hindsight Peck says he might recommend an exorcism

for Charlene). Despite their optimism, Christian writers generally maintain a belief in the darker side of human beings, or
original sin. The insistence that we are each born with disposi-
tions and personalities is a common theme, which partly under-
lies traditional religious opposition to psychoanalysis. It chose
nurturance over nature in explanations of human behavior,
religious writers complain: conceiving of every infant as tabula
rasa, psychoanalysis absolved people of ultimate responsibility
for their acts, blaming their parents instead. Psychoanalysts
were also accused of ignoring the destructive force of individual
will — they chose instinct over will, Fulton Sheen asserted —
not to mention Satan.

What popular religious writers don't recognize is that the
human will unaided can also be a force for good. Peck says
that good, healthy people are those who "do what God wants
them to do rather than what they would desire."[31] But perhaps
goodness is a matter of maintaining your own sense of what
is right, not God's, and marrying it to what you want to do.
Perhaps goodness is the marriage of principle and desire. Believers, like Peck, essentially agree, but they add that only God
can lead us to the altar. (It's just that, as Fulton Sheen said,
His suggestions are almost imperceptible, so we don't feel we're
being led.) Of course, faith in the mere possibility of being good
without God is fundamentally irreligious. If there is goodness
without God, then religion is, at best, a fairy tale; at worst,
it corrupts people with lies. "Religion is only good for good
people," Mary McCarthy said.[32]

It is probably neither reasonable nor realistic to expect popular religious writers even to entertain the possibility of godless
people being good. (Harold Kushner, a rabbi, does admit that
atheists may be good, but they can't be happy.) Instead, goodness is presented as proof that God exists. Goodness proves
His grace, and grace proves the futility of human striving. In

Peace of Mind Joshua Liebman describes the self as an achievement, but the popular Protestant writers would probably disagree. Out of popular teachings about salvation by grace the self emerges as a kind of liability, a burden to be shed, a cage to be transcended; grace is the blessing that saves us from the cursed self.

Focusing on grace, popular Protestant literature offers readers not only the promise of salvation but the assurance that they need not push themselves too hard or fret about their failures. "Grace says you have nothing to give, nothing to earn, nothing to pay," Charles Swindoll writes in *Grace Awakening*.[33] This reminder that you cannot earn God's love duplicates, or is duplicated by, the recovery movement message that a good parent loves you unconditionally; and discussions of grace are blended with popular psychology as religious writers address what they claim is the special problem of burnout and perfectionism among Christians striving to be good but feeling bad. You have to love yourself as your neighbor, almost everybody says. You have to love yourself in order to receive God's grace.

Self-esteem is hardly an original theme for self-help writers today, and perfectionism is part of what more secular or, at least, nondenominational writers consider the disease of codependency. Twelve-step groups are filled with people bemoaning their drive to be perfect, low self-esteem, and the "shaming" behavior of their abusive parents. "Christians can be such shamers!" Swindoll remarks,[34] shamelessly borrowing some jargon.

Christians are said to be particularly prone to burnout and perfectionism because of their ethic of service, not to mention their high moral standards. But Christians also have a special cure for stress and overachieving, and when they aren't psychologizing about the perils of gracelessness, the experts are upbeat about the promise of grace, which has the appeal of what is otherwise condemned as permissiveness. For too long we've been surrounded by too many "do's and don't's," Charles Swindoll says,[35] offering readers freedom from strict rules about behavior. Not that Swindoll is loathe to set down rules about belief: the doctrine of salvation by works is heresy, he proclaims. But his focus is on the liberating power of realizing you are not held accountable for your deeds, only for your willingness to believe; you need not — cannot — justify yourself or work your way to heaven: "In fact, the individual whose track record is morally pure has no better chance at earning God's favor than the individual who has made a wreck and waste of his life."[36]

If some people find this comforting, others will think it is grossly unfair. That the doctrine of grace can excuse, encourage, or at least trivialize bad behavior is a familiar charge. The equally familiar reply is that people who embrace Christ and are blessed with grace naturally behave well. But the promise of salvation extends, of course, to sinners who come to Jesus late in life, without much time left for good behavior, which may arouse resentment in their victims or other people who sinned less. Charles Stanley has the salve for this: not everyone in heaven is equal, he explains in *Eternal Security*, envisioning heaven as a sort of fiefdom in which people who led good lives are aristocracy and sinners are the serfs.[37]

Popular proponents of grace rarely consider its conceivable inequities, however, or feel the need, as Stanley does, to assure us that God is fair. Swindoll would probably condemn the concept of a fair God as an Old Testament legalism: Grace means no good deeds go rewarded while no bad deeds go punished. The good news is that God isn't fair.

Legalism, which Swindoll associates with Judaism, is one of his favorite diabolisms, along with intellectualism and humanism — a belief in the efficacy of human endeavor. Writing about "this Satanic pressurized system we call the *world*,"[38] Swindoll partakes in the traditional evangelical disdain for worldly activity that has been tempered in recent decades by the religious right's political activism.

He partakes even more passionately in the tradition of anti-intellectualism, describing reason as a barrier to faith and including among his favorite targets intellectuals, academics, and the Ivy League. To express disdain for religious pluralism, he mocks what he calls "the Harvard approach" to spreading God's word: "The thinking behind this method is: *Let's discuss all the world's religions.* Since it's *reason centered* it attracts both genuine and pseudo-intellectuals . . . no one ever gets saved!"[39] Some most likely get damned, if Swindoll is right about intellectualism and the problem of "secularism" of which it is a part. He sees "secular thought" as a dangerous virus from which Christians are not immune: "Many a believer has surrendered his mind to the world system. . . . Humanism, secularism, intellectualism, and materialism have invaded our thinking."[40]

Swindoll would vigorously deny the obvious — that he encourages readers not to think. It's true that he bemoans the decline of reading, but that's a little like a pornographer bemoaning the decline of moral values. Swindoll only wants readers to think as he does, and as Christ did before him. Like a Maoist, he lays down rules about proper and improper or subversive thinking; for him the enemy within is "European liberalism, with its subtle narcotic of humanism and socialism."[41]

If intellectualism is a sin, Swindoll is a virtuous man. His books are disorganized, derivative collections of anecdotes, platitudes, complaints about modern life, and frequent evocations of scripture. Chatty, colloquial, and not always grammatical, Swindoll is the Andy Rooney of conservative Christian preachers. "Yourself, yourself, yourself. We're up to here with self!" he announces,[42] sounding just like Rooney declaring that he's sick and tired of digging through the Crackerjacks to find the prize. Swindoll's carefully cultivated common man image is at the center of his books. He presents himself as a plain-talking, commonsensical, amiable, and virile preacher, taking care to tell us several times that he is an ex-marine. He is a muscular Christian, a "champion of purity," an archetypal nineteenth-century Protestant American male.

He's also anti-Semitic. Hebrews were "religious but not Godly,"[43] legalistic but also, Swindoll implies, hypocritical: If they considered God's relationship to man a bargain, a deal, they failed to keep their end of it. The Hebrews whom God let out of Egypt were a "thankless crowd," always complaining and incapable of faith, even in the face of miracles like the parting of the sea. I'm not sure how God felt about their skepticism, but Swindoll, for one, "cannot excuse their forgetting [His] unconditional promise."[44] In another discussion of "the Exodus crowd," Swindoll suggests that the Holocaust was a kind of recompense for turning away from God, a "warning" of where idolatry, carnality, and other sins may lead you — to Dachau, I guess.[45]

Oh well, no writer can please everyone, and Swindoll does make clear that his books are intended for Christians; in fact, he makes most of his intentions clear repeatedly. Swindoll has a genuine talent for assembling the same book several times, blending the popular cultural wisdom of the moment with his religious beliefs into "bite size chunks . . . we don't gag on."[46] Sometimes the results are bizarre. In his collection of inspirational writings, *Come Before Winter*, he blithely mines the sacred and mundane in random sequences of inspirational sound bites. One instant he's talking about sleeping in church; then he's delivering thirty-second sermons about jealousy, determination, and the problem of witchhunting. After some platitudes about living with pain, he lists twenty-five character traits "generally found in creative, innovative people." All this appears in a book that's billed as advice for people in times of stress and sadness; Swindoll is not one to be bound by a theme. Between bites about "Tough Days," and "Why Do We Suffer," he offers advice about how to write Letters of Reference.

Maybe he's simply postmodern. Like a newscaster who can recite an update on world hunger and fashion trends between commercials without segues, Swindoll shifts from the existential to the practical, devoting as much time and passion to such topics as "remembering names" as he does to his views on salvation.

Maybe no topic is too small for God's attention. Religious writer Gordon MacDonald takes aim at wasting time. Every minute we have must be used wisely (*"Time must be budgeted!"*) in order for us to enjoy a "God pleasing lifestyle," in order for us to grow. "Unseized time will flow in the direction of one's relative weakness."[47] Disorderliness is not quite sinful, but sin, MacDonald reminds us, is a kind of disorder. We must organize within for Christ, who shouldn't have to dwell amid our messes.

MacDonald relies less on scripture than does Swindoll and more on popular psychology. (Sometimes scripture is an occasion for psychologizing: John the Baptist had good parents, we're told.) Bad people, or, rather, "driven" people "gratified only by accomplishment," had bad parents and suffered *"early experience[s] of serious deprivation or shame."* MacDonald borrows recovery techniques, as well as jargon; he recommends "journaling," a popular twelve-step technique, to help you hear God speak. He also talks a lot about his own struggle to order his inner world, as recovery authors talk about their struggles with addiction.[48]

MacDonald seems to have a genuine passion for organization, considering it serious business indeed: "A disorganized spirit often means lack of inner serenity." He's a schoolmarm:

"The Christian who wants to grow will always take notes when sermons are being preached or Bible classes are being taught," we are told;[49] not taking notes is wasting time.

In this quest to manage time, MacDonald is aided by an apparent obsession with categorization, which makes him a natural self-help writer. He loves making lists, devising labels, dividing the universe into neat, knowable component parts. He's more taxonomist than theologian. The private world, for example, can be neatly divided into five sectors, which conveniently divide his book *Ordering Your Private World*. Sector one is Motivation; sector two is Use of Time; sector 3 is Wisdom and Knowledge; sector four is Spiritual Strength; sector five is Restoration. Prayer should also be organized; MacDonald has a system:

> In order to systematically pray around the world, I have divided up the continents in such a way that I can pray for each one of them: Sunday, Latin America; Monday, Central America; Tuesday, North America; Wednesday, Europe; Thursday, Africa; Friday, Asia; and Saturday, the nations of the Pacific.[50]

I imagine MacDonald as one of those people with a very neat desk. I imagine too that having organized it so well, the world must seem quite manageable to him. But something went awry, something fell out of place, because his third book in this series is called *Rebuilding Your Broken World*. In it, MacDonald confesses to adultery and chronicles his repentance and reordering. "I am Gordon and I am a sinner," he announces in the AA tradition. He tells us about the evil he discovered in himself, while exploring his inner space. He can't obliterate the evil (it's original sin), but he can manage it. Soon he is listing the four sources of temptations, four principles of rebuilding, and seven ways to defend against sin. All's right with the world once again.

While MacDonald counsels adulterers, James Dobson helps out adulterees — mostly women whose husbands have strayed — as well as the wives of batterers and alcoholics. Dobson, host of a popular radio show, is a Christian family counselor, a psychologist, not a minister, by profession, but the Bible is his bellwether. *Love Must Be Tough*, his recent book on troubled marriages, is like a sacrilized "Can This Marriage Be Saved" column in a woman's magazine.

In the self-help tradition, Dobson uses anecdotes about marital conflict to illustrate his rules about resolving it. Women should not appease their errant husbands. Instead, "the vulnerable spouse" — who always seems to be the wife — should "*open the cage door and let the trapped partner out!*"[51] Call his bluff. Love is tough.

It is a little disquieting to imagine women blindly applying Dobson's general rules to their idiosyncratic situations, but that is what self-help readers do. It is even more disquieting to contemplate the stereotypes on which Dobson's rules are based: all marital conflicts are essentially alike only if all people are too. In Dobson's world, wives nag, sometimes facilitating their own abuse: "I have seen women belittle and berate their husbands until they set them aflame with rage," he writes. Husbands are seduced by beautiful divorcees: "We must never underestimate the power of sexual chemistry existing between an attractive, needy, available woman and virtually any man on the face of the earth." Women fall into adultery not out of lust but because they feel neglected by their husbands.[52]

Maybe some of Dobson's readers run true to type. Maybe some are helped by his advice. Dobson himself seems a stereotype, with predictable prejudices about the evils of modern American life. He prefaces a discussion of homosexuality with this warning: "CAUTION: SENSITIVE INFORMATION FOLLOWS . . . If you have a weak stomach or don't wish to know the more unpleasant facts about homosexuality, I encourage you to skip the remainder of this section." He disdains feminism, the "so-called woman's movement," for teaching women selfishness and turning them away from God. He disdains women, assuming that they are malleable creatures who need to be fed the right programs. Summing up the "New Woman," he says, "her new system of values has been programmed for her by feminist organizations and publications almost as though a computer software package were keypunched into her brain."[53]

Children also are creatures to be tamed, in Dobson's view. *Dare to Discipline*, a primer on child rearing, presents the parent-child relationship as a series of power plays. Defiant children, under ten, should be spanked: "Pain is a marvelous purifier . . . the spanking should be of sufficient magnitude to cause the child to cry genuinely." To discipline older children, remember that "the shoulder muscle is a surprisingly useful source of minor pain."[54]

Dare to Discipline was written in 1970 before there was much public concern about child abuse. But in his attitudes toward children Dobson is no slave to fashion. In his 1987 book, *Parenting Isn't for Cowards*, he still endorses corporal punishment, and he is still preoccupied with breaking strong-willed children, driven by a "raw desire for *power*."[55]

For Dobson there are essentially only two types of children — compliant and willful (guess which he prefers), and he begins *Parenting Isn't for Cowards* with a report on his own parent poll about compliance and willfulness: Strong-willed children outnumber compliant children by about two to one; they are stressful, hard to handle, and ultimately less likely to succeed. Compliant children are better students who are more likely to become well-adjusted adolescents and successful adults.

These "facts" are interesting only as indications of Dobson's prejudices; the poll from which they were gleaned seems worthless. The terms *compliant* and *willful* were not defined. Parental labeling of children was purely subjective as were parental assessments of their children's success as young adults. In the self-help world, however, a poll like this is what passes for scholarship and helps give Dobson an aura of expertise.

But Dobson doesn't really need empirical evidence that willfulness is bad or at least problematic; for him, that's an article of faith. A child who rebels against his parents is more likely to rebel against God, and Dobson stresses that strong-willed children especially must be taught about "divine accountability"; they must be taught that God's laws are enforced: "The wages of sin is death and children have a right to understand that fact." Dobson fondly recalls his own mother's teachings about "heaven and hell and the great Judgment Day when those who have been covered by the blood of Jesus will be separated eternally from those who have not."[56] In Dobson's book, God believes in tough love too.

If this unabashed authoritarianism is currently out of vogue, it does provide a measure of the fist inside the velvet glove of grace. If God is portrayed as the perfect parent of recovery literature, He is still a parent who expects to be obeyed. Grace entails the promise of forgiveness only if we come round in the end. (It's not too late, preachers on 42d Street proclaim into their microphones, but someday it will be.) Dying in disbelief, we risk damnation. Given this omnipresent threat of dreadful retribution, God's well-publicized expectation that we obey Him out of love, not fear, seems a little unrealistic.

Believers might reply that loving obedience can only be experienced, not imagined or explained — although explaining is precisely what self-help writers aim to do. Moreover, to question the possibility of obedience without fear is to question the larger religious ideal of loving self-surrender, which popular Christian writers tend to present as fairly easy.

David Seamands, at least, admits that it is hard. "Self-surrender is the ultimate crisis because it represents the ultimate spiritual battle," he advises. "It may take a long time to travel from conversion to self-surrender."[57] Seamands describes surrender of the will to Christ the way addiction experts describe recovery — as a process, not an event. You can promise to be guided by God's will ever after; but you must carry out that promise day by day.

Seamands focuses on the barriers you encounter along the way, between conversion and surrender, familiar barriers such as "the perfectionist complex." He calls it "the most disturbing emotional problem among evangelical Christians" (self-help writers like hyperbole); perfectionism is characterized by "tyranny of the oughts . . . self-depreciation . . . anxiety [and] legalism. . . ." The cure, of course, is grace, or rather the "process of growth in grace."[58] The causes include "unpleasable parents" and "unpredictable home situations."

Like M. Scott Peck and the Minirth-Meier authors, Seamands is a Christian counselor, offering instruction in psychology as well as religion. Indeed, his basic message too is that mental and spiritual health are entwined: "The mechanisms of our personalities which we use in faith are the same instruments through which our feelings operate." Religious dysfunction, then — atheism or a belief in salvation by works — is attributed to psychological dysfunctions, such as paranoia or low self-esteem, which are attributed to dysfunctional families and Satan. Low self-esteem is "the most powerful psychological weapon that Satan uses against Christians."[59]

Seamands thus neatly reconciles religion and psychology and provides his Christian audience with what may be genuinely helpful, simple, commonsensical lessons about personality development and the relationship of temperament to faith. He is not as relentlessly self-aggrandizing as his colleagues, or competitors, so the lessons seem more sincere. They are also more interesting because Seamands ventures into what could be dangerous ground — the psychoanalysis of religious belief — except that he only psychoanalyzes disbelief.

Bad relationships with God derive from bad relationships with parents, or, as Seamands says, Christians with "damaged love receptors" can't receive God's love and distort His character, presuming Him to be untrustworthy, critical, and "unpleasable," like their parents. This is more or less conventional wisdom in popular Protestant literature, but Seamands elaborates on it, with some thoughtfulness, recognizing that what you tell people about God is "filtered through" their personalities. He concedes that "the facetious remark — 'Man creates God in his own image' — contains an element of truth."[60] What he does not and perhaps cannot consider is the possibility that a "healthy" Christian outlook reflects temperament and conditioning too — not truth.

Whether you analyze faith or the lack of it probably depends on whether you are one of the faithful. The intellectual effort to explain or categorize, to "lay bare the causes" of attitudes and beliefs, is essentially hostile, as William James observed; it is a "method of discrediting states of mind for which we have an antipathy."[61] But as James also pointed out, faith reflects a willingness, a capacity, to believe: "Our belief in truth itself . . . that there is a truth, and that our minds and it are made for each other, — what is it but a passionate affirmation of desire?"[62] The truths we choose are also functions of our temperament, and some temperaments are unable to believe in any truth at all; some "never are [or] could be converted."[63]

It is the failure of popular Protestant writers to recognize this — that some people are temperamentally incapable of Christian belief — that I find most troubling, particularly in the context of their views on salvation. In the end we are saved by belief and damned by the lack of it, even if we live well and try hard to believe but cannot. *"The Holy Spirit* does not condemn us because we have failed to be good. He convicts us, says Jesus, 'about sin, because men do not believe in Me.' Grace brings us to the place of *real guilt,* real guilt for our only sin — failing to believe in Jesus Christ and trust Him for right-relatedness to God."[64]

As an article of faith, this doctrine of salvation by grace and grace alone is remarkably unappealing to me. It takes, I think, remarkable disregard for justice to idealize a God who so values belief over action. I prefer the God who looks down on us, in a very old joke, and says, "I wish they'd stop worrying about whether or not I exist and start obeying my commandments."

It is possible to posit moral standards in a godless world? Most popular religious writers don't even raise the question, although they answer it implicitly, blaming modern immorality on god-lessness. Harold Kushner, at least, considers the possibility of ethical humanism before rejecting it, devoting his most recent book to the subject of Who Needs God? (we do, of course). Faith in some god, one god, is essential to our construct of a moral world, he concludes. Like the Protestant writers, Kushner associates godlessness with moral relativism: without God, matters of morality become mere matters of "personal taste," he warns.[65] But he doesn't fully acknowledge that our tastes in God are personal and idiosyncratic too. It is as diffi-cult for us to agree about the nature of the one true God as it is for us to reach consensus on hard questions like abortion. What difference does God make?

Kushner addresses our deep divisions about God mostly by denying them, claiming, in the end, that we have a shared sense of injustice that comes from God. Our differences are differences in detail, he might say, and Kushner is tolerant of different approaches to God: "Religions can disagree and still each be true."[66] He describes a sort of moral umbrella of monotheism, not insisting on the superiority of any particular denomination.

Like M. Scott Peck, Kushner speaks to a broad, nondenominational audience, with vaguely articulated questions about God, or simply a sense of existential unease. His best-selling book, *When Bad Things Happen to Good People*, offers an accessible reading of the Book of Job that will comfort people who don't like imagining God as a bully. Evil exists because God is powerless to eradicate it, he suggests. (In *Peace of Mind*, Joshua Liebman offers a similar explanation of evil.) Kushner is refreshingly critical of the platitudes inflicted on people who sustain terrible losses: Losing your children or being crippled in a senseless accident is not simply "for the best." Evil cannot be rationalized or made sacred. God grieves with us over injustices that He can only give us strength to bear.

Not everyone will find solace in this view. It requires that you give up a belief in God's omnipotence and in the notion that everything happens for good reason. It requires you to believe in randomness, the possibility of inexplicable bad luck. A lot of us prefer to believe in sin, original or derivative, regarding evil as moral recompense or karma. Kushner's notion of evil is a challenging one; it presents us with a universe that even God cannot entirely control.

Uncertainty, however, is not what we seek in religion, and Kushner assures us in his most recent book, *Who Needs God?*, that the universe is ordered and purposeful after all. Or, at least, he has chosen to believe that it is. "We seem to *need* to see the world as one that makes sense," he observes,[67] as if our need for God proves He exists. Popular religious writers often assume that mystery itself proves God. M. Scott Peck points to recoveries he can't explain as signs of grace, as if whatever he doesn't understand is holy.

To describe religion as wishful thinking is not to deny its usefulness or power. Faith can be self-fulfilling: to leap across an abyss, you are better served by faith than doubt, James stressed.[68] Or, as Kushner says with less eloquence but equal conviction, "You become a certain kind of person when you choose to believe that there is a pattern and purpose to the universe. . . . Certain things seem worth making the effort to do, and others seem less scary. . . . And both you and the world are better off."[69]

Like most self-help writers, Kushner does sometimes seem to be talking to children. He is a laborious writer, the kind who quotes an Oscar Wilde epigram and then explains it. His style is familiar; he relies on the usual anecdotes about people he's counseled and references to popular culture (self-help writers invoke television shows and popular songs the way academics invoke Foucault). His most popular book is also partly confessional. Kushner tells his own story about the tragic death of his son in *When Bad Things Happen to Good People*, which is an interesting book because there's anger and uncertainty in it — the shadow of a spiritual crisis. "It is all right to be angry at God," Kushner says.[70]

He still offers many of the same, familiar messages found in popular Protestant literature. He denigrates self-sufficiency, American individualism, and competitiveness, and celebrates community. (Americans do penance by buying books that criticize the way they live.) He talks about the importance of self-esteem, asserting that "one of the goals of religion is to teach people to like themselves and feel good about themselves."[71] But Kushner does present a different vision of God and a different model for our relationship with Him.

We can be angry with God and we can argue with Him. We are not called so strongly to submit. *"Obedience is not necessarily the highest religious virtue,"* Kushner suggests. "God is mature enough to derive pleasure from our growing up, not from our dependence on Him.... [Religion] should call upon us to grow, to dare, even to choose wrongly at times and learn from our mistakes rather than being repeatedly pulled back from the brink of using our own minds."[72] Kushner suggests that although God makes moral demands on us, we are actively engaged with Him in shaping ourselves and our world.

Some will call this heresy or hubris; some will simply find it unsatisfactory. It is not a terribly popular image of God (I'm not even sure Kushner endorses it). The notion that our relationship with God is, in part, collegial qualifies the ideal of self-surrender with self-reliance — with the image of Moses walking up Mount Sinai.

■ ■ ■

Alienation and anomie aside, there are worse credos for a participatory democracy than the belief that actions matter. Nineteenth-century liberal Protestantism may have been materialistic, imperialistic, and naive about the power of men, and an occasional woman, to shape their environments, but at least they were encouraged to try. Now popular religion, like a twelve-step group, reminds us that we're powerless.

What's missing in much popular religious literature today is a model for ethical action in the world. Focusing on the individual relationship with God, on the state of individual belief, while disparaging individualism, most popular religious writers offer no thoughtful discussion about moral behavior, giving us no basis for community. Practicing their own brand of legalism, they offer a laundry list of moral wrongs — abortion, homosexuality, adultery, atheism, and rebellion — but no guidance in resolving moral dilemmas. Harold Kushner at least offers some comfort, acknowledging the pain of placing your aging parent in a nursing home, suggesting that one goal of religion is to help us find peace when we have made "honest, painful choices about our lives." M. Scott Peck pays some attention to citizenship, calling generally for grass-roots, community-oriented activism. But people convinced of their own helplessness as individuals don't come together in democratic companionship; they come together as mobs, bereft of both self and community.

Conclusion: The Political Problem of Self-Help, Which the Author Has No Idea How to Solve

"What makes man a political being is his faculty of action," political theorist Hannah Arendt wrote.[1] Losing faith in your own willfulness and capacity to act, you eventually lose freedom. That was one lesson of totalitarianism, which succeeded by organizing masses of disaffected, politically inactive, self-centered people who felt helpless and victimized, believed they didn't matter, and sought "self-abandonment" in the state.[2] The recovery movement and other popular religious revivals today are hardly analogs to Stalinism or Naziism, any more than the United States in the 1990s is analogous to Weimar Germany. Recovery is not a regimented, political movement and does not demand total loyalty from its followers; for many recovering persons, recovery is only a part of life, not the whole.

But an apolitical movement that helps shape the identities of a few million people will have political consequences, and the ideology of recovery makes me question what those consequences might be.

What are the political implications of a mass movement that counsels surrender of will and submission to a higher power describing almost everyone as hapless victims of familial abuse? What are the implications of a tradition that tells us all problems can be readily solved, in a few simple steps — a tradition in which order and obedience to technique are virtues and respect for complexities, uncertainties, and existential unease are signs of failure, if not sin? The notion of selfhood that emerges from recovery (the most vulgarized renditions of salvation by grace, positive thinking, and mind cure) is essentially more conducive to totalitarianism than democracy.

The dangers of exalting universally applicable techniques over individual analysis, or instinct, are probably self-evident; even self-help experts deny that they believe in "quick fixes," right before offering them. The dangers of will-lessness and submission are obvious as well, and recovery experts regularly deny that they encourage dependence. The popularity of victimhood has been noticed and bemoaned, but it remains a rich subject for sociologists and political scientists. Like contestants on "Queen for a Day," Americans of various persuasions assert competing claims of victimhood, vying for attention and support. The intense preoccupation with addiction and abuse reflects an ominous sense of powerlessness that infects gender and race relations, and notions of justice and heroism, as well as our view of the self.

What a self-help expert would call our victim syndrome is perhaps most apparent, and most remarked on, in racial conflicts. As I write this, Orthodox Jews and blacks in the Crown Heights section of Brooklyn are at war over respective claims of victimization, each feeling brutalized by history and the other. The Tawana Brawley case, involving false allegations of racially motivated rape, demonstrated most dramatically the uses of victimization as a political ploy. Long after her story about being raped by members of the Ku Klux Klan was discredited, Brawley and her advisers, Al Sharpton and C. Vernon Mason, visited the Central Park jogger gang rape trial to "observe the differences in the court system between a white and black victim."[3] Comparing Brawley to a woman who was, in fact, raped, beaten, brain damaged, and nearly killed, Sharpton and Mason exploited a pervasive sense of victimization among blacks that is almost matched by a sense of victimization among whites. The racist populism of Jesse Helms and former Klansman David Duke and the rage that periodically erupts in racial murders feed on white resentment of affirmative action and the political empowerment of minorities, just as Willie Horton ads fed on white fear of black crime.

Who's doing what to whom? Distinguishing victims from oppressors seems merely a matter of perspective. Tawana Brawley reportedly concocted her tale of rape in order to explain her absence from home, to appease an abusive stepfather. With different spokespersons, putting a different spin on her story, she could have been a feminist cause célèbre.

Read as a parable of either race or gender, the Brawley case delineated the appeal of victimization. Not only may victimization make you famous and the center of some small circle of attention, it offers absolution and no accountability and creates entitlements to sympathy, support, and reparations. As putative victims of racism, prosecutorial abuse, crime, or codependency, people like Marion Barry, recovering former mayor of Washington, D.C., and New York subway vigilante Bernhard Goetz can be self-righteous instead of remorseful, outraged instead of ashamed, and guilty of nothing but maybe a bit of bad judgment.

Of course, conflicting claims of victimization are often at the center of criminal cases, whether defendants allege they're being prosecuted unfairly or that they were driven to crime by drugs, mental disorders, or post-traumatic stress. What's remarkable about our notion of victimhood today is its inclusiveness and its spread beyond the courtroom's structured exchange of accusations. Smokers are the victims of tobacco companies, troubled teenagers are the victims of rock and roll, alcoholics are the victims of their genes, and a support group for the "Victims of Plastic Surgery" claims 3,500 members. Women still feel victimized by men and men feel victimized by feminism; blacks and whites feel victimized by each other, and nearly everyone feels victimized by some ill-defined assemblage of crooks and incompetents who looted the savings and loans, as well as by their dysfunctional families. With the rise of a personal development movement centered around victimization, victimology can fairly be called the study of our culture.

Not that recovery is entirely to blame. The cultist fascination with victimhood that fuels the recovery movement and may account for its success is complicated and partly rooted in political changes dating back to the 1960s: Warren Court decisions expanding the rights of people accused of crimes helped spawn a populist victim's rights movement. Feminism and the civil rights movement underscored the historic victimization of women and minority males, demanding change that eventually made some white males feel like victims too. In its campaign against affirmative action, the Reagan administration adopted the language of victimization, focusing its enforcement efforts on the "white male victims" of "reverse discrimination." Feminism engendered a men's movement and demands for men's rights. As rich white guy movie star Michael Douglas explained, "Guys are going through a terrible crisis right now because of women's unreasonable demands."[4]

The men's consciousness movement, our newest major personal development craze, celebrates the victimization of middle-class males. "Men are suffering right now — young men especially," Robert Bly announces,[5] blaming men's suffering partly on (who else?) their mothers. He charges women with belittling their husbands and encouraging boys to disrespect their fathers. There is a clear strain of misogyny in the men's movement: Bly suggests that the way for men to deal with disagreeable women is to "bust them in the mouth."[6] But the fervor with which masses of middle-class whites have responded to Bly's message about the alienation of men from their fathers also suggests some inarticulate, covert resentment of the attention recently paid to the absence of father figures in poor, African-American communities. Bly's mythopoetic piety lends his laments about fathering an air of profundity: fathers have been "immersed in demonic darkness," he explains.[7] Still, his complaints about the workaholism and emotional weakness of middle-class fathers are less compelling than the problems of children with no fathers at all, mothers with no partners, and young African-American males who are less likely to survive into adulthood than their white counterparts. Only recently has Bly acknowledged the crisis of men in the African-American community.

The recovery movement, from which the men's movement branched, offers similar sanctification to the complaints of middle-class people who resent being preempted by the pressing problems of the poor. In recovery, whether or not you were housed, schooled, clothed, and fed in childhood, you can still claim to be metaphorically homeless. (John Bradshaw's television series offers you "Homecoming.") Your inner child is a displaced person, lost and alone. At its worst, the recovery movement's cult of victimization mocks the notion of social justice by denying that there are degrees of injustice. It equalizes

all claims of abuse, actual and metaphoric. The personal sub-
sumes the political, with dire consequences for both politics
and personality development.

In this dysfunctional society of victims, where everyone has
a legacy of abuse, and every abuser was once a victim too, paranoia is perfectly logical: it's a way of being well adjusted. That
the specter of child abuse may haunt the unconscious — it
sometimes makes amnesiacs of its victims — is a paranoiac's
delight. To be a victim you don't need to remember your abuse;
you need only imagine it.

Truth is highly subjective to people whose central experience
is victimization: the details, the facts of any particular instance
of oppression, don't matter to those who are sure of their oppression in general. If Al Sharpton were ever to admit that Tawana
Brawley's story was a lie, he might claim, like a fiction writer,
that it told a deeper truth: If Klan members hadn't attacked
Brawley, they'd surely attacked some other young black woman,
sometime, somewhere. If law enforcement officials weren't cover-
ing up crimes in the Brawley case, they'd surely covered up other
crimes against black people, at other times and places. If whites
are collectively guilty of oppressing blacks, then guilt may be
assigned to individual whites arbitrarily, as arbitrarily as oppression has been meted out to blacks.

It is a perverse form of justice that devalues truth and makes
individual guilt and innocence irrelevant. "Where all are guilty,
no one is," Hannah Arendt wrote.[8] Or, as the savings and loan
crisis showed, when everyone's guilty, there's no one to blame.
As Arendt also pointed out, a disregard for facts combined
with certainty of belief is what gives mass propaganda its power.
For politically disaffected people who suspect that "every statement [is] a lie anyhow," the truth is simply what one chooses
to believe.[9]

This willingness of people who feel victimized and out of control to believe anything or nothing hardly makes for responsible political leadership. Everyone knows that campaign slogans are lies, so many people who may have voted for George Bush in 1988 because of his no-new-taxes pledge didn't seem particularly indignant when he broke it. What Arendt called a "mixture of gullibility and cynicism"[10] also tempered public reaction to the Iran-Contra affair. Voters didn't seem to mind terribly that administration officials lied about the war in Nicaragua or efforts to trade arms for hostages. People who don't take responsibility for their own actions or addictions don't seem to expect much responsibility from their leaders. "Shit happens," bumper stickers proclaim. "Mistakes were made," President Reagan remarked, leaving us to wonder who made them.

Truth in this world is as arbitrary as the bureaucracy that makes victims of us all. Anyone who has ever stood in line at the motor vehicle bureau or argued with a clerk about a traffic ticket knows what it is to feel powerless. Being recognized as a victim is at least affirming. Surviving as one is heroic. When action is no longer possible, heroes are people who wait.

Perhaps this is another legacy of the Holocaust. It severed the tenuous connection between action and experience. If genocide can be understood, it can't be rationalized. To its victims who do nothing to provoke it, except exist, genocide is wholly arbitrary, like terrorist attacks on airports or bystander shootings in the Bronx. So the Holocaust gave us as heroes "survivors," victims who endured the worst and emerged with immeasurable moral authority, for which many compete today. Seeking the sanctity of victimhood, with cynicism or hysteria, antiabortion activists routinely claim that abortion is a holocaust, which must make every newborn a survivor. To recovery experts, childhood itself is a holocaust. Still, internment in a concentration camp is a level of victimization that is hard to match, although many do, as the litany of human rights abuses worldwide shows. Stateless people, AIDS victims, and people trapped in poverty in urban war zones claim their right to be remembered too.

It isn't that suffering shouldn't be recognized and avenged, not that it shouldn't evoke awe as much as its infliction evokes outrage, not that survival doesn't require shrewdness and strength as well as luck. But if we valued action or believed in it, if we felt the world was even partly of our making, we'd treat victims with compassion and respect but not reverence. The cult of victimhood reflects a collective sense of resignation. It responds to widespread feelings of helplessness in the face of poverty, crime, disease, pollution, bureaucracy, taxes, deficit spending, technology, terrorism, and whatever else composes the crisis of postmodernity. It is the posture of people in a Kafkaesque world of accidents, anonymous authority, and no explanations, a world in which language loses the power to make sense and character hasn't much to do with fate.

This belief in the individual's irrelevance is hardly a basis for a free society or a compassionate one that responds to individual suffering. It is hard to fashion a rational, secular response to pervasive feelings of powerlessness that will keep participatory democracy alive. You can offer only modest answers: a suspension of disbelief (act as if your actions matter), a tolerance for limited expectations of some justice, and the self-respect to do what is right for its own sake. Confronted with their own incapacity to act, people are more likely to seek refuge in nihilism, totalitarianism, authoritarian religious fundamentalism and the wait for Armageddon, or a sunnier belief in the dawn of a New Age (Don't Worry, Be Happy). Or they put all their faith in the power of the isolated self. Instead of giving in to victimhood, they deny it.

A blinding fear of what can't be controlled probably accounted for the popularity of Werner Erhard's est, repackaged as The Forum. Erhard's philosophy offers people the myth of total control, assuring them that everything they do matters, that they are each wholly responsible for themselves and wholly in charge of their destinies. That this makes no one responsible for anyone else and quickly devolves into victim blaming is probably also part of its appeal. In this world of winners, people take all the credit for success and all the blame for failure, as if good fortune reflected a good moral character and bad fortune a weakness of will: you are the hero of your own life and no one else's.

Erhard's vision is as terrible as Kafka's, and after the Holocaust it is surely less true. Nor is it particularly heroic. Whether the individual means everything or nothing, we have no model of heroism — if heroism includes empathy and some concern for justice — and without a model of heroism we have no model of citizenship. Erhard's philosophy absolves you of a social conscience, as victimhood robs you of a sense of purpose.

It takes a great leap of faith or the purest integrity to persist in taking actions that seem hopeless. In the 1960s and 1970s, activism was fueled by a belief in its own efficacy, a feeling that we were happening to the world as much as it was happening to us. "It was fun to have that sense of engagement where you jumped on the earth and the earth jumped back," Abbie Hoffman recalled.[11] His belief in the force of protest may have been only a little more realistic than his efforts to levitate the Pentagon (in 1968, in Chicago, he claimed, protesters "destroyed the two party system in this country and perhaps with it electoral politics"),[12] but at least it was energizing. Now even college students seem tired politically or bored, if not nihilistic, as Hoffman complained. The challenge for their generation is to discover "how you struggle for social change without having

any hope," he said in a speech at the University of South
Carolina shortly before his suicide. "I wouldn't know how to
fight from that particular stance."[13]

■   ■   ■

There is a Kafka parable about a man, K, who seeks admit-
tance to the Law. The gate to the Law is open, but a gatekeeper
denies him entry, with the warning that he is only the lowliest
gatekeeper; there are others, more powerful, along the way. K
believes he should have access to the Law but does not challenge the gatekeeper or try to slip past him. Instead he sits down
before the gate, pleading with the gatekeeper, bribing him in
vain, and watching him incessantly for many long years, the
rest of his life.

"Never ask permission," I once took the moral to be. "Never
settle for a low-level no," a friend suggested, remembering what
he'd learned on his first day at Harvard over twenty years ago.
But K sits and waits, and in the end he is an old man talking
to the fleas in his fur collar, begging the fleas to get the gatekeeper to let him in.

This parable is told by a priest in *The Trial*. K is being tried
for a crime that is never revealed to him, by an omnipotent
court with no discernible rules. At first K tries to argue, to
reason with the Court, but, like a man in quicksand, the more
he struggles the deeper he sinks. Verdicts are always inevitable,
he learns. His guilt is not just presumed; it's assigned.[14]

You can read this as an argument for faith and calm acceptance of passivity. Maybe K should have done nothing. Maybe
trusting the Court would have saved him. You can read it as an
argument for nihilism — "Curse God and die," Job's wife tells
him, while he's complaining that God isn't fair. Or you can
read K's story as a cautionary tale about the perils of victim-

hood, the perils of choosing blind faith or nihilism, the virtues of leaving some dilemmas unresolved.

There are, however, no dilemmas like this in recovery, where higher powers are always entirely benign and faith is not in general a subject for debate. Today, Kafka would be considered terminally codependent — overwhelmed with shame (the legacy of his abusive, "shaming" father) and cut off from his "feeling reality" (he was always intellectualizing). A recovering person interpreting K's story would probably dismiss it by saying that K was thinking with his head and not his heart, pointing out that you cannot reason your way to faith or recovery.

But if faith is by nature profoundly irrational, it is also inadequate as a guide to worldly affairs. Perhaps you cannot reason your way to faith, but neither can you base political as well as personal choices solely on revelation, as recovery's ideology might encourage you to do. There are, of course, many reasonable people in recovery, but the movement itself so discredits reason that it seems like just another symptom of codependency. Rational, left-brain thinking is generally associated with "denial." Not that the recovery movement is wholly responsible for the denigration of reason. Personal development movements in America tend to be anti-intellectual: mind cure and positive thinking chose faith over reason too.

In this respect the personal development tradition is more religious than secular. The emphasis on personal, emotional experience, or sensation, was the mark of nineteenth-century American Protestantism. Pietism, the individualistic, "intuitive religion of the heart," was exalted by revivalist movements that pervaded "practically all the denominations."[15] One result of a "flight from 'reason'" by the churches was a flight of intellectuals from the churches. According to historian Sidney Mead, "Americans since 1800 have, in effect, been given the hard choice between being intelligent according to the prevailing standards in their intellectual centers or being religious according to the standards prevalent in the denominations."[16]

Personal development movements have been even more consistently hostile to intellectuals than the churches Mead describes, and they have perversely combined the anti-intellectualism of the pietistic tradition with a myth of expertise. Self-help consumers may idealize intuition, but they tend to rely on experts. And, looking outside themselves for guidance on how to be, they're encouraged to view the world solely in terms of its effect on the self. The measure of any political or social event, as well as any relationship, is how it makes you feel.

Unconfined to the spiritual realm and bereft of any genuine appeal to intuition, pietism is reduced to a passive solipsism that threatens political freedom. The "mass man" organized by the Nazis and merged into the state, Hannah Arendt observed, was the man who would "sacrifice everything — belief, honor, dignity" to maintain his own security. There is surely a lesson for acolytes of recovery in this: "Nothing proved easier to destroy than the privacy and private morality of people who thought of nothing but safeguarding their private lives."[17]

It is one of the oddities of American culture that heightened concern for private interests — the "selfism" of recovery — can coincide with the devaluation of privacy. People want to talk about themselves, but in groups or on TV. It is perhaps an irony of history that in 1990, as Eastern Europe and the Soviet Union seemed to be moving toward democracy, we may have been unwittingly eroding its foundation — a view of ourselves as active, willful political beings. I can't help wondering if the personal development ethos is contagious. Shortly after the aborted August 1991 coup by hardliners in the Soviet Union, which occurred while I was immersed in this book, I dreamt that I attended a raucous session of the Russian Parliament to observe the beginnings of democratization. People were denouncing the Communist party, reciting its crimes with much specificity, until a woman presiding over the session leaned into her podium and said, "Enough facts, my friends. Tell us how you feel."

■   ■   ■

I waver between being amused by personal development movements and disturbed by them, which, in the end, seems appropriate. Borrowing blithely from so many sources — psychology, religion, positive thinking, and the presumption that Americans are entitled to be happy — the recovery movement, for one, may be too confused ideologically to ever pose a serious threat. The personal development tradition in general is rife with inconsistencies and outright contradictions. Pietism coexists with pragmatism: the primacy of feelings is rivaled only by the primacy of techniques. Individualism coexists with obeisance to the crowd: the drive for individual fulfillment is rivaled, and maybe surpassed, by the desire to conform. Perhaps this only mirrors the contradictions in American democracy itself, which has, I remind myself, survived two hundred years of self-help and will probably survive a few more.

The packaging of conventional wisdom about personality development, spirituality, family life, success, and gender roles as self-help reconciles American ideals of choice and individualism with the reality of majority rule and a hunger to belong. Eager for rules on how to be an individual, Americans consume millions of self-help books every year, choosing from an array of experts as wide as the array of TV dinners. Eager for company and social acceptance, they form support groups to make sure the quest for self-actualization isn't lonely. Glorifying the power of individuals to shape their own identities, they seek experts, gurus, guidance from someone, anyone, other than themselves.

The self-help industry exploits its readers' fears of being singular, if singularity means embarking on the search for self alone. In doing so, it performs a political function. Self-help literature tends to ensure that the selves readers find or make are standardized and socially congenial. The potentially disruptive quest for individual identity is collectivized.

The perverse relationship between popular notions of self-actualization and self-effacement is most clearly delineated by cults: selves are actualized by obedience, worship of a higher self, and submersion in a regimented, insular collective. This does not mean that every self-help consumer is a potential Moonie or that every expert is obsessed with power. Cults are at the extreme end of a continuum, beginning with support groups, that most people don't traverse; and many exercises in personal development seem too silly to be dangerous. Exploring your past lives with Shirley MacLaine or chanting a twelve-step mantra with your support group may be fairly harmless entertainments. But there is a relationship between the hunger for rules on individual development, inspiring the silliest self-help fads, and the abdication of individual responsibility; that relationship is dramatized by cults.

To criticize the conformity implicit in self-help you needn't deny the solace people find in collectivity or suggest that they are better off pursuing their bad habits individually than reforming them in groups. You needn't question the sincerity of recovery proselytizers or even the benefits offered by a few profiteers: we are all better off if self-proclaimed addicts consume only books. We will all survive recovery. But what of the passivity and search for simple absolutes the recovery movement reflects? The putative message of codependency literature — that we are responsible for ourselves and shouldn't spend our lives pleasing or heeding others — is undermined by the medium in which it is conveyed. Merely buying a self-help book is an act of dependence, a refusal to confront the complexities of a solitary creative act and to endure the loneliness and failures that are the price of its surprises.

What I miss most in the self-help tradition is a spirit of improvisation. For all their talk about intuitive, "feeling realities," experts rely on readers' willingness to surrender not just rationality but intuition, by which they might lead themselves to unsuspected places. Experts exalt intuition, but they don't actually value it. How could they? It would threaten their business much more than intellectualism ever has or could.

Imagine America without self-help books. Imagine everyone grappling with their problems and forging their identities, using their own intuitions and powers of analysis and maybe some help from their friends. Imagine that. I can't. I have no cure for America's self-help habit and no advice to offer on how to find one. (This is what publishers disparage as a "negative" conclusion to a book.) I have no expectations that the "problem" of self-help ever will be solved. Instead, I expect more self-help books, not less, now that publishers have a broad new market to exploit — wanna-be-"wild" middle-class men.

Codependency books may soon be as passé as last year's diet, but the self-help genre will always be in fashion. Self-help books market authority in a culture that idealizes individualism but not thinking and fears the isolation of being free. "A book must be the axe for the frozen sea within us," Kafka wrote. Self-help is how we skate.

Notes

Introduction

1. Sigmund Freud, *Civilization and Its Discontents* (New York: Norton, 1961), 49.
2. Robert A. Becker, *Addicted to Misery* (Deerfield Beach, Fla.: Health Communications, Inc., 1989), 60.
3. Beverly DeAngelis, *Secrets About Men Every Woman Should Know* (New York: Delacorte Press, 1990), 156.
4. Edwin McDowell, "What Students Read When They Don't Have To," *New York Times*, July 9, 1990, sec. c, p. 16.

ONE — Chances Are, You're Codependent Too: Recovery

1. "Co-Dependency: A Special Report from the First National Conference" (Deerfield Beach, Fla.: U.S. Journal Training, Inc., 1989).
2. Melody Beattie, *Codependent No More* (New York: Harper & Row, 1989), 31.
3. "Co-Dependency: A Special Report," 6.
4. Conversation with Peter Vegso, Health Communications, Inc., December 1989.
5. John Bradshaw, *Bradshaw On: The Family* (Deerfield Beach, Fla.: Health Communications, Inc., 1988), 43, 26.
6. Ibid., 10.
7. Ibid., 77.
8. Charlotte Davis Kasl, *Women, Sex and Addiction* (New York: Ticknor & Fields, 1989), 31.

9. Anne Wilson Schaef, *Co-Dependence: Misunderstood — Mistreated* (New York: Harper & Row, 1986), 35.

10. Bradshaw, *Bradshaw On: The Family*, 47.

11. Anne Wilson Schaef, *When Society Becomes an Addict* (New York: Harper & Row, 1988).

12. Schaef, *Co-Dependence: Misunderstood — Mistreated*, 67.

13. Schaef, *When Society Becomes an Addict*, 5.

14. Carla Wills-Brandon, *Is It Love or Is It Sex?* (Deerfield Beach, Fla.: Health Communications, Inc., 1989).

15. Lynne Namka, *The Doormat Syndrome* (Deerfield Beach, Fla.: Health Communications, Inc., 1989), 152.

16. Jeremiah Abrams, ed., *Reclaiming the Inner Child* (Los Angeles: Tarcher, 1990), 1.

17. Melody Beattie, *Codependent No More*, 114–115.

18. Bradshaw, *Bradshaw On: The Family*, 236.

19. Harlan J. Wechsler, *What's So Bad About Guilt?* (New York: Simon & Schuster, 1990), 170.

20. Namka, *The Doormat Syndrome*, 75.

21. Norman Vincent Peale, *The Power of Positive Thinking* (New York: Fawcett Books, 1952).

22. William G. McLoughlin, *Modern Revivalism* (New York: Ronald Press, 1952).

23. Ibid., 84.

24. See Stanton Peele, *The Diseasing of America* (Lexington, Mass.: Lexington Books, 1985).

25. Bradshaw, *Bradshaw On: The Family*, 92.

26. Ibid., 199.

THREE — Don't Worry, Be Happy: Positive Thinking to est

1. Peale, *The Power of Positive Thinking*, 70, 20, ix.

2. Norman Vincent Peale and Smiley Blanton, *Faith Is the Answer* (New York: Fawcett Books, 1950), 28.

3. Peale, *The Power of Positive Thinking*, 70, 30.

4. Ibid., 33, 127, 122.

5. Ibid., 29, 124.

6. Ibid., 124.

7. Ibid., 125.

8. William James, *The Varieties of Religious Experience* (New York: Penguin Books, 1985), 87.

9. Ibid., 95.

10. Ibid., 96, 163.

11. Donald Meyer, *The Positive Thinkers* (Middletown, Conn.: Wesleyan University Press, 1965), 279.

12. Peale, *The Power of Positive Thinking*, 65, 94.

13. Ibid., 100.

14. Ibid.

15. Ibid., 157.

16. Ibid., 135.

17. Ibid., 134.

18. Napoleon Hill, *Think and Grow Rich* (New York: Fawcett Books, 1960).

19. Ibid., 15, 16.

20. Ibid., Publisher's Preface.

21. Ibid., 53.

22. Ibid., 29.

23. Ibid., 49.

24. Ibid., 67.

25. Ibid., 214.

26. Mark Twain, *Christian Science* (Buffalo, N.Y.: Prometheus Books, 1986), 44.

27. Mary Baker Eddy, *Science and Health* (Boston: Christian Science Publishing, 1906), 97.

28. Twain, *Christian Science*, 72.

29. Meyer, *The Positive Thinkers*, 77.

30. Abraham H. Maslow, *The Farther Reaches of Human Nature* (New York: Penguin Books, 1971), 13, 24.

31. Abraham H. Maslow, *Toward a Psychology of Being* (Princeton, N.J.: Van Nostrand Reinhold, 1968), 155.

32. Ibid., 21.

33. Ibid., 10.

34. Ibid.

35. Maslow, *The Farther Reaches of Human Nature*, 9.

36. Maslow, *Toward a Psychology of Being*, 159.

37. Ibid., 79.

38. Ellen Herman, "Being and Doing: Humanistic Psychology and the Spirit of the 1960s," in Barbara L. Tischler, ed., *Sights on the Sixties* (New Brunswick, N.J.: Rutgers University Press, forthcoming).

39. Maslow, *The Farther Reaches of Human Nature*, 57.

40. Quoted in Herman, "Being and Doing: Humanistic Psychology and the Spirit of the 1960s."

41. Maslow, *Toward a Psychology of Being*, 57.

42. Abbie Hoffman, *The Best of Abbie Hoffman* (New York: Four Walls Eight Windows, 1989), 42.

43. Ibid., 41.

44. Herman, "Being and Doing: Humanistic Psychology and the Spirit of the 1960s."

45. Maslow, *The Farther Reaches of Human Nature*, 7.

46. Joyce Brothers, *How to Get Whatever You Want Out of Life* (New York: Ballantine Books, 1978).

47. Ibid., 1.

48. Ibid., 28–31.

49. Ibid., 48–51.

50. Ibid., 44.

51. Ibid., 145.

52. Ibid., 57–58, 62, 157.

53. Ibid., 146–147.

54. Ibid., 163–169.

55. Ibid., 96.

56. William Warren Bartley III, *Werner Erhard* (New York: Potter, 1978), 167.

57. Ibid., 62, 108, 147.

58. Barbara Grizzuti Harrison, *Off Center* (New York: Dial Press, 1980), 197–220.

59. Bartley, *Werner Erhard*, 199.

60. Harrison, *Off Center*, 206.

61. Eddy, *Science and Health*, 207.

62. James, *The Varieties of Religious Experience*, 362.

FOUR — In Step: Support Groups

1. "Clean and Sober — and Agnostic," *Newsweek*, July 8, 1991, 62–63.
2. Trish Hall, "New Way to Treat Alcoholism Discards Spiritualism of AA," *New York Times*, December 24, 1990, sec. A, p. 1.
3. "Clean and Sober — and Agnostic," *Newsweek*.
4. I am quoting Nancy Rosenblum, paraphrasing Conor Cruise O'Brien.
5. "Unite and Conquer," *Newsweek*, February 5, 1990, 50.
6. Richard F. Mollica, "The Trauma Story: The Psychiatric Care of Refugee Survivors of Violence and Torture," in Frank M. Ochberg, ed., *Post-Traumatic Therapy and Victims of Violence* (New York: Brunner/Mazel, 1988), 297, 309–310.
7. Richard F. Mollica and Russell R. Jalbert, "Community of Confinement: The Mental Health Crisis in Site Two," The World Federation for Mental Health, February 1989, 14.
8. Ibid.

SIX — Stop Making Sense: New Age

1. Shirley MacLaine, *It's All in the Playing* (New York: Bantam Books, 1988).
2. Stephen R. Covey, *The Seven Habits of Highly Effective People* (New York: Simon & Schuster, 1989).
3. Twain, *Christian Science*, 21.
4. Ibid., 70.
5. Covey, *The Seven Habits of Highly Effective People*, 47.
6. Ibid., 48–49, 52.
7. Michael Lewis, "Every Man a Milken," *New Republic*, October 29, 1990, 16.
8. Will Nixon, "The Flight from New Age," *Publishers Weekly*, December 7, 1990, 32.
9. "Programs," Werner Erhard & Associates, 1989.
10. Richard Leviton, "Meditation Goes High-Tech," *East West*, March 1990, 57.
11. Nixon, "The Flight from New Age," 21.
12. Ibid.
13. Ibid., 23–24.

14. Ibid., 26–30.
15. Robert Bly, *Iron John* (Reading, Mass.: Addison-Wesley, 1990).
16. Ibid., 98, 249.
17. Jack Thomas, "Following the Beat of a Different Drum," *Boston Globe*, August 21, 1991, 43.

SEVEN — God Is a Good Parent Too: Self-Help and Popular Theology

1. M. Scott Peck, *The Road Less Traveled* (New York: Simon & Schuster, 1978), 172.
2. M. Scott Peck, *The Different Drum: Community Making and Peace* (New York: Simon & Schuster, 1988), 123.
3. James Dobson, *Love Must Be Tough* (Dallas: Word Publishing, 1983).
4. David Seamands, *Healing for Damaged Emotions* (Wheaton, Ill.: Victor Books, 1981), 11.
5. Charles Swindoll, *Come Before Winter and Share My Hope*, (Wheaton, Ill.: Living Books, 1985), 406.
6. Robert Hemfelt, Frank Minirth, Paul Meier, *Love Is a Choice* (Nashville: Thomas Nelson, 1989), 277.
7. See Katy Butler, "Spirituality and Therapy: Toward a Partnership," *Utne Reader*, January/February 1991, 75–83.
8. Fulton Sheen, *Peace of Soul* (New York: Whittlesey House, 1949), 70.
9. Peck, *The Road Less Traveled*, 223
10. M. Scott Peck, *People of the Lie* (New York: Simon & Schuster, 1983), 83.
11. Peck, *The Road Less Traveled*, 16, 77, 279.
12. Peck, *People of the Lie*, 205.
13. Peck, *The Road Less Traveled*, 267, 270.
14. Peck, *The Different Drum*, 176.
15. Peck, *The Road Less Traveled*, 44, 22, 81.
16. Peck, *People of the Lie*, 78–79, 83.
17. James Dobson, *Parenting Isn't for Cowards* (Dallas: Word Publishing, 1987), 89.
18. Charles Swindoll, *Improving Your Serve* (Dallas: Word Publishing, 1982), 83, 84.

19. Peck, *The Different Drum*, 240.
20. Ibid., 288.
21. Sheen, *Peace of Soul*, 188.
22. Peck, *People of the Lie*, 258.
23. Peck, *The Different Drum*, 130.
24. Ibid., 124.
25. Peck, *The Road Less Traveled*, 170, 171.
26. Peck, *People of the Lie*, 154, 155.
27. Ibid., 173.
28. Ibid., 159.
29. Ibid., 176.
30. Peck, *The Road Less Traveled*, 163.
31. Peck, *People of the Lie*, 78.
32. Mary McCarthy, *Memories of a Catholic Girlhood* (New York: Harcourt Brace, 1946), 23.
33. Charles Swindoll, *Grace Awakening* (Dallas: Word Publishing, 1990), 87.
34. Ibid., 231.
35. Ibid., xv.
36. Ibid., 25.
37. Charles Stanley, *Eternal Security* (Nashville: Thomas Nelson, 1990).
38. Swindoll, *Come Before Winter*, 114.
39. Ibid., 148–149.
40. Swindoll, *Improving Your Serve*, 133.
41. Swindoll, *Come Before Winter*, 164.
42. Swindoll, *Improving Your Serve*, 39.
43. Charles Swindoll, *Strengthening Your Grip* (Dallas: Word Publishing, 1982), 197.
44. Charles Swindoll, *Dropping Your Guard* (New York: Bantam Books, 1987), 35, 38.
45. Swindoll, *Strengthening Your Grip*, 199, 200.
46. Swindoll, *Improving Your Serve*, 48.
47. Gordon MacDonald, *Ordering Your Private World* (Nashville: Thomas Nelson, 1984), 68, 75.
48. Ibid., 31, 45.
49. Ibid., 116, 111–112.

50. Ibid., 156.
51. Dobson, *Love Must Be Tough*, 45.
52. Ibid., 150, 16.
53. Ibid., 164, 159.
54. James Dobson, *Dare to Discipline* (Wheaton, Ill.: Living Books, 1970), 16.
55. Dobson, *Parenting Isn't for Cowards*, 110.
56. Ibid., 106, 107.
57. David Seamands, *Putting Away Childish Things* (Wheaton, Ill.: Victor Books, 1982), 122, 125.
58. Seamands, *Healing for Damaged Emotions*, 79–93.
59. Ibid., 117, 49.
60. David Seamands, *Healing of Memories* (Wheaton, Ill.: Victor Books, 1985), 100–103, 97.
61. James, *The Varieties of Religious Experience*, 11–12.
62. William James, *The Will to Believe* (New York: Dover, 1956), 9.
63. James, *The Varieties of Religious Experience*, 204.
64. David Seamands, *Healing Grace* (Wheaton, Ill.: Victor Books, 1988), 137.
65. Harold Kushner, *Who Needs God?* (New York: Pocket Books, 1989), 71.
66. Ibid., 196.
67. Ibid., 32.
68. James, *The Will to Believe*, 59.
69. Kushner, *Who Needs God?*, 34.
70. Harold Kushner, *When Bad Things Happen to Good People* (New York: Avon Books, 1981), 108.
71. Kushner, *Who Needs God?*, 198.
72. Harold Kushner, *When All You've Ever Wanted Isn't Enough* (New York: Pocket Books, 1986), 127, 132.

Conclusion

1. Hannah Arendt, *Crises of the Republic* (New York: Harcourt Brace Jovanovich, 1972), 179.
2. Hannah Arendt, *The Origins of Totalitarianism* (New York: Harcourt Brace Jovanovich, 1973), 305–389.

3. Ronald Sullivan, "Police Said to Ignore Warnings on Jogger Suspect," *New York Times*, July 31, 1990, sec. 2, p. 3 (photo caption).

4. Quoted in Susan Faludi, *Backlash: The Undeclared War on American Women* (New York: Crown, 1991), 121.

5. Bly, *Iron John*, 27.

6. Faludi, *Backlash*, 310.

7. Bly, *Iron John*, 100.

8. Arendt, *Crises of the Republic*, 162.

9. Arendt, *The Origins of Totalitarianism*, 382.

10. Ibid.

11. Hoffman, *The Best of Abbie Hoffman*, 382.

12. Ibid., 65.

13. Ibid., 402.

14. Franz Kafka, *The Trial* (New York: Schocken Books, 1974), 213–215.

15. Sidney Mead, *The Lively Experiment: The Shaping of Christianity in America* (New York: Harper & Row, 1963), 125–130.

16. Ibid., 129.

17. Arendt, *The Origins of Totalitarianism*, 338.

Index